Next of Kin Next Door

How to Find Sasquatch
a Stone's Throw Away

Christopher Noël

The only thing I can compare it to is being mentally reborn. Nearly everything I thought I knew has been given a different slant. Once I dropped what I expected of these people, an entire culture was opened up to me. What I am able to tell you so far is this: These are a people who do not want to be "found." These people fit in with us like gears. What we lack, these people possess. What these people lack, we possess.

> —an East Texas Sasquatch
> witness quoted in *Our Life with Bigfoot*

If I ever go looking for my heart's desire again, I won't look any further than my own backyard.

> –Dorothy Gale in *The Wizard of Oz*

Also by the Author

Sasquatch and Autism: Twelve Parallels

Mindspeak: Tapping into Sasquatch and Science

*A Field Guide to Sasquatch Structures: The 50
    Most Common Types in North American Forests*

The Sasquatch Savant Theory: Three Books in One

The Girl Who Spoke with Giants (novel)

*Our Life with Bigfoot: Knowing Our Next of Kin
    at Habituation Sites*

Table of Contents

Part 1

Micro Forests, Greenbelts, River Corridors, and Ravines: Ten Case Studies from across North America

Part 2

The Nature of the "Beast": Who are They and Why Can't We Meet Them?

Part 3

How to "Talk" to the Neighbors: Connoisseurs of
Concrete Thinking

Part 4

"I've been zapped!" An Electric Connection?

Part 5

The Nearness of You: Anthropology in a New Key

Preface

> What I've found down in the river bottoms in the city
> is just as impressive as, if not more than, all the stuff
> that I've found in the mountains. It is absolutely
> incredible how far these guys can come in and remain
> undetected. (Nathan Reo, Utah Sasquatch)

Obviously, Sasquatch are not everywhere, but they are far more numerous, widely distributed, and, in some cases, much closer at hand than we have so far grasped. Their territory honeycombs our own.

The project to prove this fact is, however, an uphill climb. So counterintuitive is the notion, for most, that Sasquatch can exist at all that to venture any further claims about their nearness—how they routinely invade our geographical "bubble"—is bound to fall on deaf ears at first. We need a wholesale revolution in our thinking.

Yet the truth is the truth, and in the near future, the fundamentals of this kindred species, including its sheer *right-thereness*, will be recited matter-of-factly by every first-grader, even if most will never see a Sasquatch in their lifetime. We'll all know *of* them as we do ultraviolet light, Earth's magnetic field, or the elements—as a presence both concrete and abstract, to be accepted implicitly on good authority.

Some wonder, Why expose a race of wild people who clearly wish to remain hidden? Why can't we just leave them alone? My answer is two-fold.

> 1. Because they are real and because more and more
> people are seriously studying them, the discovery and
> general acknowledgement of this species is 100%

inevitable, whether this occurs next Thursday or twenty-five years from now;

2. Given this fact, our most vital goal needs to be to make sure the world gets reliable information during the transition process, information that correctly frames public understanding so that disastrous misinformation ("They are monsters! Shoot them on sight!") can be deflected, defeated, or held to a bare minimum. I expand on this issue in the video "Is it Morally Wrong to Seek Sasquatch?"

For the past half century, since the Patterson-Gimlin Film, the prevailing viewpoint has been that, if the species exists at all, it must be very thinly distributed, subsisting in small nuclear family and clan groups.

The leading proponent of this scarcity argument is Dr. Jeffrey Meldrum, the Idaho State professor of physical anthropology who has broken from the mainstream paradigm and leaned against significant professional headwinds to rigorously analyze the evidence and vouch for the legitimacy of this field of hominin inquiry. Meldrum makes a ballpark population estimate of fewer than five thousand Sasquatch across North America. He further proposes that most adults probably lead "solitary lives."

I esteem Dr. Meldrum highly, but on both counts he is plainly incorrect. In addition to ranging very far from human civilization centers, this species also ranges very near, as this book will demonstrate. This fact points to a total continental population in the hundreds of thousands. Also, abundant eyewitness accounts hold that where there is one Sasquatch, there are many; they coordinate socially in tactical units. I would bet my life that there are far more than five thousand in Idaho alone.

If even this most high-profile and enlightened spokesperson for Sasquatch reality finds some of the basics highly implausible, society at large will require even heavier persuasion.

A related myth that will need to be knocked down is that Sasquatch research requires extreme penetration into the wild. Currently, Todd Standing is the prime example of this macho mindset; in order to have a chance of encountering the species we must, he believes, thrust ourselves deep, deep into remote territory. His promotional videos are forever touting the top researchers he has "guided into the hardcore backcountry wilderness of North America!"

Standing on expedition

In truth, as we will see, Sasquatch also operate in softcore frontcountry…and plentifully. If you not only read this book but also watch the recommended videos, you will get the full picture.

To reach a tipping point in our collective consciousness will demand a broad-based cultural shift, which will in turn demand the combined energies of many.

Fortunately, this movement is already gaining steam. Everywhere we turn these days, talk of Sasquatch proximity is in the air. A prime recent example is the December 7, 2017, episode of the "Bigfoot Crossroads" podcast, entitled "Bigfoot in the City" (YouTube). Listen especially from 7:23-16:33 (about Chicago); from 24:01-33:16; from 35:08-41:00 (about Tulsa, OK, South Haven, MS, and Des Moines, IA); and from 47:14-50:39 (about Ottumwa, IA, and Jefferson City, MO). Co-host Coonbo Baker—

one of our great, colorful characters and a walking encyclopedia of eyewitness accounts—puts it this way:

> I mean, really and truly, right around any big city has become a pretty good place to research because you've got everything they need. Like the Army, they adapt and overcome. They're learning to live off of our food sources. Throw me down in any large city and I can root around and find some Boogers [Sasquatch]. You look where your green areas are and there's a high probability you're going to find some there.

My own small-town Vermont version of this "throw me down in any" approach can be seen in my videos "Taking the Random Forest Challenge" and "Sasquatch & Serendipity: How Three Lucky Breaks Taught me Where to Find Them" (YouTube channel Impossible Visits).

The fifteen cases featured in Parts 1 and 3 of this first edition could well be multiplied a hundred-fold, and I'd like to begin that process immediately. That's why I'm asking for your help, for contributions from anyone with evidence that confirms and builds upon what's presented in this book. You can contact me at NextofKinNextDoor@gmail.com. Have you noticed structures in your back yard, on the outskirts of town, or in greenbelts or ravines running right through your city or suburb? Have you recorded wood knocks or vocals? Have you even caught our shadowy neighbors on camera, not far off? With permission, over the months and years ahead, I will include your supplemental material in regular updates, thickening the book until fewer and fewer can find reasons to doubt that our next of kin are, indeed, busy leading their lives alongside us—some of them just a stone's throw away.

Christopher Noël
Northeast Kingdom, Vermont
January 1, 2018

PART 1

MICRO FORESTS, GREENBELTS, RIVER CORRIDORS, AND RAVINES
TEN CASE STUDIES FROM ACROSS NORTH AMERICA

1. Montpelier, Vermont—Population 8000

For years, I was aware of occasional visits to my home in northern Vermont, as documented in Chapter Eight of *Sasquatch Rising 2013* and in the video "Sasquatch on the Home Front." And then, in August and September of 2014, I interacted daily with a group of them in a ravine just two miles away; see the video "Morning Visits 2014." (Note: Whenever I refer to a video in this book, it will be available on YouTube.)

2015 was a far less dramatic year, except on August 17 when—for just four seconds and unwittingly—I filmed a juvenile hiding behind a small pine tree; see "Morning Visits 2015: The Juvenile Sasquatch Footage."

But I live in very rural country, homes and small villages surrounded by hundreds of square miles of undeveloped forest, so while I was surprised and delighted, of course, to find the species within close range, I had no reason to radically change my sense of where they live: They live in the woods, sometimes venturing briefly to the edge of human civilization, sometimes even making oblique contact with us, but then retreating to the wilderness.

It wasn't until May 9 of last 2017 that the full weight of Sasquatch proximity—of the exact and startling degree to which their territory and ours can *interpenetrate*—finally landed on my thick skull. For several winter weeks, my ten-year-old daughter had been exploring the micro forest behind my mother's neighborhood in the city of Montpelier, capital of Vermont. After the snow melted, I noticed, for the first time, that the area is chock full of stick and tree structures; see "In the Micro Forest 1." There's nothing like finding clear-cut evidence of the species in one's own mother's back yard to wake a person up to reality; it was a shock of recognition. I had scoured many nearby mountains and ridges, including those with a history of sightings and wood knocks, yet never had I come across the quality and concentration of structures that I found here. To say I was flabbergasted would be an understatement. Here's a small sampling…

No, my mother has never experienced any of the typical suite of Sasquatch overtures that occur at "habituation sites," as reported by the contributors to my book *Our Life with Bigfoot*. And as far as I know, neither have her neighbors. Sometimes, our evolutionary next of kin prefer to simply keep to themselves, operating right beside us without making their presence known.

On the nights of May 9 and June 16, I placed an audio recorder in this forest and obtained dramatic results—on the first night, an obvious wood knock; on the second night, within just five hours, a "wooo" vocalization, a loud limb break, an apparent double hand-clap, and two tree pushes. Hear these on "Right Here Beside Us: Rethinking Sasquatch's Whereabouts."

For the surprising rest of my 2017 research season in the local micro forests, see Part 4.

2. Sanford, Florida—Population 54,000

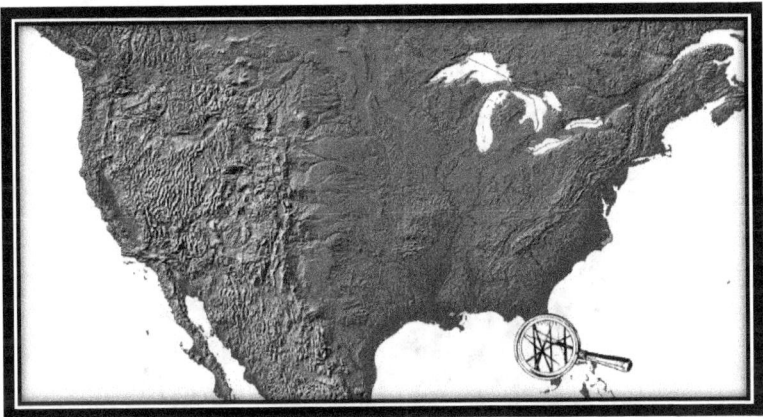

J.P. Smith's first sighting occurred behind his recording studio. There was a dense, "jungly" forest fenced off by chicken wire—a narrow swath of nature bounded, on the other side, by a main road and an industrial park. The oblong shape I've drawn shows that area of Sasquatch activity; the arrow points to the studio.

When I visited J.P. in March of 2012, we sat for hours behind his studio, late at night, and sure enough, I heard wood knocks and heavy movement over there in the darkness.

He sharead an experience he'd had a year earlier.

> Looking into this thick jungle area, I could see there
> was light behind the trees. And I could see multiple
> silhouettes just pacing back and forth behind this set of
> trees, all different sizes. There was one big, lurking
> shadow, there's always the big one. They don't show
> themselves that much but they kind of direct what's to
> be allowed. They definitely chose to show themselves
> to me at this particular time.

**J.P Smith in 2012. He is the co-author, with Freeman
Young, of an excellent book, *Communion with Sasquatch.*
Smith passed away in 2014.**

> A misconception is that they're always on the ground,
> walking around on two legs. That's not been my
> experience. The day before my sighting, I was looking
> up into the trees, and where the palm trees meet the
> great swamp oaks, the palm fronds hang over and
> make perfect little rooms, like little nests. So I started
> wondering, Could they be hanging out way up in the
> treetops? I started paying attention to that spot.

> So the next day, I went up there at about 5:30 in the
> afternoon, just before dusk, and I'm sitting near the
> fence, watching that same area, about fifty or sixty feet
> away, and I see this overhanging nest area start to
> shake. We have a lot of big birds down here, like

sandhill cranes, so I'm thinking, Could a bird be getting ready to fly up out of here? But a bird didn't fly out of it. A Sasquatch jumped from the little nest onto another palm tree, and then from that palm tree onto a great oak, right at twelve o'clock in front of me, and when he did he clung to the side of the tree but upside down. His head was facing towards the ground. He moved so unnaturally.

The closest thing I can compare it to is seeing Spiderman stick to the side of a building. He was so *fast*, man, I saw him fly from the palm tree over to the oak tree...and when I say fly I mean he *soared* across...I don't know, maybe twenty feet? Which wasn't much for him, you know. He was an adult, seven or eight feet tall, and he was all gray. So he didn't look at me or anything, he just stuck on the tree, like...you ever see a jumping spider? Jump, land, turn itself around real quick? That's how fast he turned himself right-side up. And then he quickly shuffled himself to the back of the tree and then came down. But when he moved to the back I could see his hands and his feet hugging the tree, like a tree-climber would, with spikes? But of course he didn't have any spikes. I could see his hands and feet coming down the tree, and then he just stood there, behind it. At that point, he had his back to me. He just stood there with his back to me.

This is the last thing I expected to happen, I'll tell you that much. I just couldn't believe how he moved—it's fluid, it's *so* fluid. I turned to tell somebody, but there was nobody there.

One afternoon in August of 2011, J.P. scanned the area and—without even realizing it—captured a few seconds of a young Sasquatch clinging to a treetop, about seventy-five feet off the ground. You can see head, shoulders, spine, butt, and his legs straddling the trunk. Of course, I wish the resolution were much, much higher.

On "Tree-Hugger Sasquatch: A Closer Look at Footage by J.P. Smith," through a very shaky camera, you can make out the figure quickly slipping around to the right side of the tree, at which point—surprise!—another pops out on the left side. When you see the video, you will understand why these screen grabs are of such low quality.

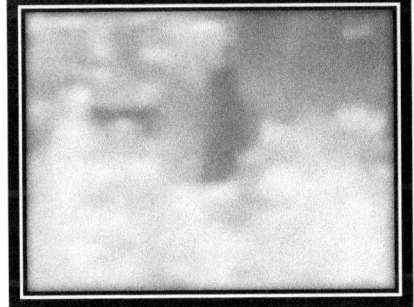

One head...   ...two heads

3. Paris, Texas—Population 25,000

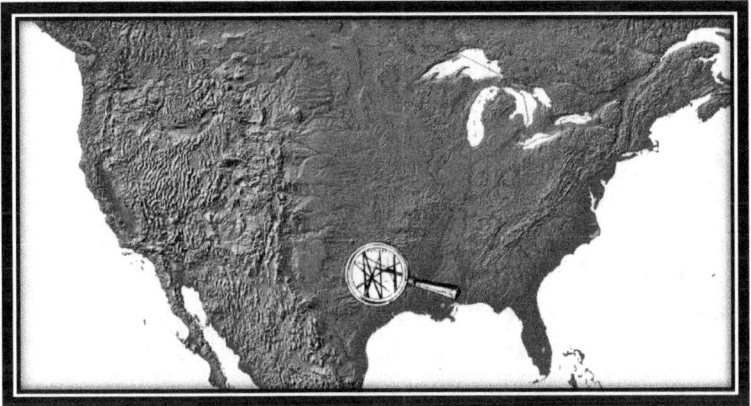

In 2002, on the outskirts of town, a property owner noticed that some heavy, discarded tires in the woods were being frequently relocated. Because some of these tires turned up in trees, Sasquatch were suspected. The owner, his wife, and three other men then entered into a systematic, two-and-a-half-year research project that yielded some of the world's most fruitful results.

First, they decided to chain those roving tires to a solid tree. To put it mildly, the subjects of the experiment didn't appreciate this ploy; see the video "M.K. Davis Revisits the Bigfoot Destroys a Tree Video."

Before...   ...after (same tree shattered)

As will be discussed in Part 2, Sasquatch will go to almost any lengths to remain unseen, but they are not infallible—not *quite*. Capturing them on video even fleetingly required the team to mount surveillance cameras around the property, eventually obtaining 1200 hours of footage, painstakingly reviewing it every step of the way, sometimes frame by frame, for thirty months. Many have tried this same basic technique to rousing failure, but in this case, the dedication paid off, eventually bringing in a priceless collection of clips, none by itself approaching the clarity of the Patterson-Gimlin film but contributing, in their totality, to a broader picture of Sasquatch behavior. In many instances, unlike "Patty," the subjects here were unaware that the camera was on them, and so we can witness what they do in the absence of a human observer.

To increase the odds of success, the team applied tremendous care and ingenuity to the process, putting together attractive groupings of toys and other objects and sometimes (brilliantly) aiming the cameras *away* from these set-ups—*but into mirrors*. You can familiarize yourself with this breakthrough technique by watching "M.K. Davis Discusses How to get a Bigfoot into Camera Range." Also fascinating in this regard is "Do Sasquatch Know what a Camera Is?"

Renowned video analyst M.K. Davis—whose major claim to fame are his unparalleled breakdowns of the Patterson-Gimlin Film—worked closely with this Texas researcher, enhancing the visual and audio quality of the clips and contextualizing them for the viewer with insightful commentary. Without Davis on board for this project, it's doubtful that we would have any of this superb evidence before us today. Davis has contributed substantially to our field of study; indeed, of the nine clips included in "The Daily Life of Sasquatch: Nine Glimpses," a compilation showing how the species behaves on its own time, when not concerned about being watched, five stem directly from Davis's talents—and three in this candid pantheon were obtained right here on this Paris property.

Here, for your enjoyment, is the cream of the crop.

1. "M. K. Davis revisits the fence climber"

2. "M.K. Davis discusses the quick glimpses video"
3. "M.K. Davis discusses the creek walker video and the unusual walk"
4. "M.K. Davis looks closely at the creek crossing in the white Bigfoot video"
5. "M.K. Davis discusses the night runner"

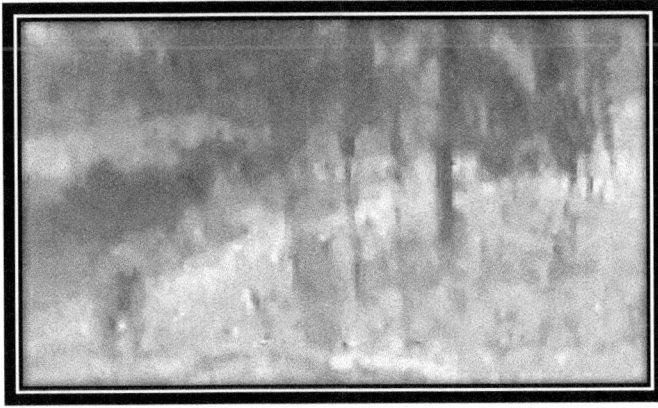

6. "M.K. Davis looks at quick clips of a white Bigfoot"
7. "M.K. Davis discusses the Sasquatch altercation video"
8. "M.K. Davis talks about size and scale in the video of an alleged Sasquatch"
9. "M.K. Davis discusses the Bigfoot in a tree"
10. "M.K. Davis discusses the white Bigfoot at the feeder video"
11. "M.K. Davis discusses video of an alleged Sasquatch that is very large"

Now we cross over into vocalizations.

12. "M.K. Davis discusses the voice in the shed video"

13. "M.K. Davis asks Does Sasquatch Mimic Human Speech?"
14. "M K Davis discusses the tire talker video"
15. "M.K. Davis discusses the crow caller video"
16. "M.K. Davis discusses the walk and talk video" (after watching this video, you should also watch "21 Degrees between Bigfoot and You," by ThinkerThunker)
17. "M.K. Davis discusses the night screamer video"
18. "M.K. Davis discusses the fast talker audio"
19. "M.K. Davis discusses vocals from a Bigfoot video"

One of the team, Warren, later moved to a larger city in Texas, where he began to apply the old Paris tactics in secluded green space.

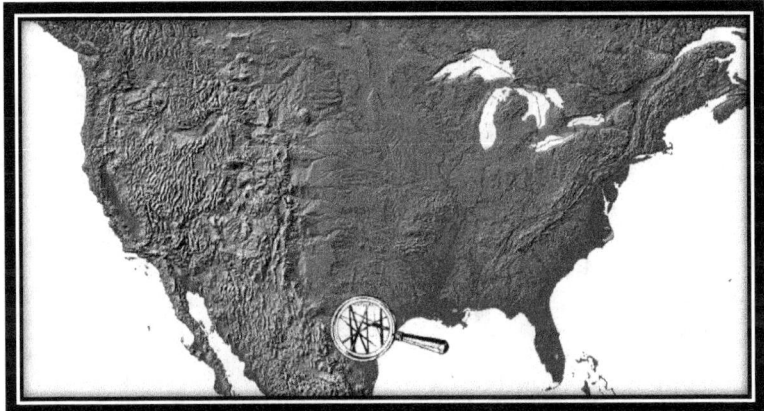

His methods are already producing results, nothing as striking as before, not yet, but he's been posting a series of blog articles called "The Urban Sasquatch Journal"; to read the entire series from the beginning, Google "The Urban Sasquatch Journal: What is Urban Sasquatch?" Warren contributes photos and notes, and the overview is written by fellow researcher Sharon Day. Here are a few excerpts.

> Certain urban settings are sort of "Sasquatch islands" where they utilize roadways, storm drains, power line roads, railroads, and other sources to move back and forth between bodies of protected lands.
> Many urban Sasquatch situations are in wildlife areas and hiking parks adjacent to businesses and residential areas. These are often civilization-locked large acreages of protected land.
>
> There is no need to fear interactions because the very same stealth utilized to remain in forests filled, say,

with campgrounds and hikers is used in urban settings as well. They no more want to get caught in such settings than they ever do in the deeper wilderness and, in fact, they have to assess the risk/reward ratio even more carefully here near us before acting.

Once a regular source of food is developed, they can sometimes become more emboldened and even annoyed if a source dries up. This same thing occurs in habituation sites when owners quit feeding them. Like anyone else, they are thankful for easy resources and get quite comfortable in this routine. Other than some tantrums, some tossing of rocks, etc., there is no reason to believe that they become more directly aggressive. Once again, their primary directive is, above all else, to not be seen.

Dumpsters facing woodlands are easy targets for "stuff," whether it's useful objects—such as cups, tarps, buckets, rope—or food. It's a rather irresistible dive.

Recesses under bridges, tucked in and protected, have been utilized, mostly in the case of remote suspension bridges. As well, storm drains have been used to get from one wooded area to another without the need to risk being seen on roadways.

Within the woods, you can often find stockpiles of "junk" in a certain area. This is often a sign of Sasquatch activity. These collections may be used to attract and ambush smaller forest animals for food. They are lures. They can't use the trash cans left in parks because they are located where people walk, but they can take that waste into the forest and make an irresistible foraging pile.

There are sightings in populated areas, often in parks on the periphery of a large metropolitan area, as well as in greenbelts. Outside of cities like Seattle, Dallas, Louisville, and others, you might find a ring of county parks that offer a combination of quiet woodlands and commuters hoping to live further from the fray. This combination leads to sightings on golf courses and cemeteries. Why these locations? Because of all the human sites, these two are least likely to be lit at night or occupied by humans and most likely to intersect a stretch of promising woodland. If they are going to do their traversing at night, these are the best areas to be out in the open at less risk.

The true concern for an urban Sasquatch is the dependence on our waste. The braver they become in coming closer and realizing this is where some good stuff is tossed, the more the situation echoes the trouble with bears in parks. This is not to say they would get aggressive like bears, but their very dependence on our cast-offs is concerning when it comes to catching our diseases and running security risks for easy food. It's been difficult enough for people to accept the concept of Sasquatch in the great wilds, but convincing them that these commandos of the forests can get closer to homes and businesses than ever imagined can be downright impossible. What you will see in this series will relieve your mind that, even in the case of a researcher repeatedly interacting, they still do not wish to show themselves in these urban settings and retain

the same skill set and survival capabilities as their
more rural counterparts.

4. Denver, Colorado—Population 600,000

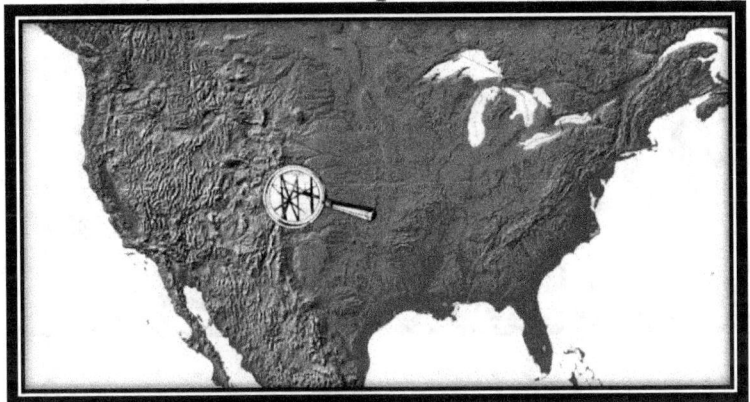

Here is a short entry, a developing case study at its outset, representative of so many others underway across North America. The researcher posts as MrDuffy81, and I especially recommend four of his videos, shot in a Denver suburb: "Urban Sasquatch Creek Structures—Bigfoot Bicycle Homage," "Lair O' the Sasquatch Neighbors," "Wildman Igloo in Suburban Treehouse Sanctuary," and "Roadside Sasquatch Structure in Colorado."

In the last video, he finds a small, intricate structure in plain sight of many homes and a main road, a wide, stamped-down path leading directly to it. Some have opined that this structure could have been built by human children, to which I say that kids wouldn't put together such a careful/artful construction, complete with telltale cross pieces, that is too small for them to get into and play inside. Nor would they gather limbs and branches from somewhere else and carry them to such a random spot. Nor would their small shoes create such a path. I bet that in the summer, this location is well hidden by surrounding grass.

The image below comes from "Urban Sasquatch Creek Structures." We can see a city street in the background and a rider mower in the midground.

Within earshot of traffic, the researcher comes across multiple Sasquatch structures, asking rhetorically, "Who really does this…stacking up sticks all weird?"

5. Vail, Colorado—Population 5300

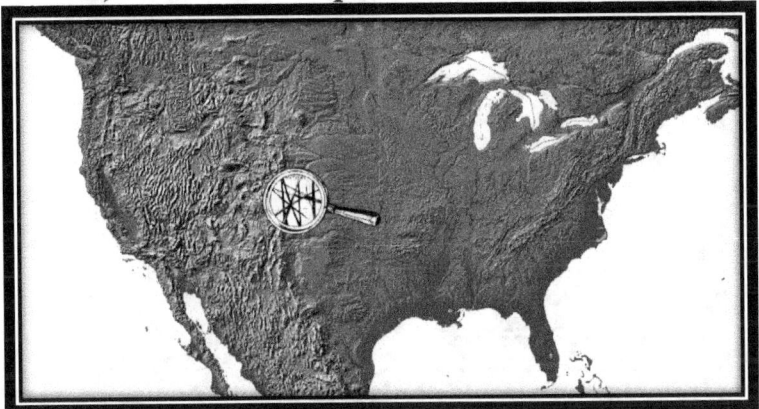

For the past two years, Mark Abell has been accumulating a loyal YouTube audience by documenting the spectacular structures he finds deep in the forests, nowhere near human trails. He also records wood knocks and vocalizations here.

By way of comparison, here is a structure photographed by researcher Tracey Allred just outside of Casper, Wyoming.

For striking "best of" reels, take a look at "Bigfoot Confirmed on Video, Stills, Worlds" and "Bigfoot Confirmed 2" (from the 4:25 mark onward).

The reason I am featuring Abell's research in this book is that he also finds elaborate structures very close to civilization. One would certainly suspect human involvement if these neighboring constructions, hiding in plain sight, didn't so perfectly match what he has filmed in extremely remote areas. See my video "Appreciating Colorado Bigfoot 1: Much Closer than we Imagined," in which he discovers blatant evidence within sight of roads, buildings, biking trails, and snowboarding runs.

This structure was found within sight of Vail Resorts; see "Vail Bigfoot Wigwam."

For further discussion of Abell's work, see Part 2.

6. Hartford, Wisconsin—Population 14,000

Sasquatch reports have emerged less than four miles from where the 2017 US Open golf tournament was held. Here's an example.

> A man contracted by the Department of Natural
> Resources to pick up road kill came to the Washington
> County Sheriff's Department to report a 7-foot-tall
> "animal" had taken a deer out of the back of his pickup

truck at about 1 a.m. Thursday, Sheriff Brian Rahn said.

According to the report, the man loaded a deer carcass into the back of his truck on Highway 167 near Station Way, got into the cab, and prepared to drive away when a large black animal, very wide and larger than a bear, jumped into the back of his pickup and dragged out the carcass he had just loaded.

"He was horrified and took off out of there," said Rahn. (*Greater Milwaukee Today*, 2006)

In the exact same area, a researcher I know (who prefers to remain anonymous) has recently discovered forest structures and has recorded wood knocks in the middle of the night. Take a look at the video "Sasquatch in the Rough."

7. Hamilton, Ontario—Population 552,000

Since 2010, a researcher named Jim has been steadily posting videos as TimberGiantBigfoot. He lives on the outskirts of Hamilton and explores a forest accessed by well-maintained public trails.

He often rides his bicycle to his research locations.

He has conducted fruitful, dedicated research, recording vocals, wood knocks, tree pushes, and documenting structures of wood and stones.

Jim beside an early structure in 2010

Jim's son

He often finds stones mounted in the crooks of trees and stacked into small towers.

Two structures found within 20 feet of each other

One day, he parked his bicycle against a tree, checked for changes in this familiar neck of the woods, and gathered some wild leeks. He heard voices and footsteps just out of sight, which he pursued for a while, saying on the video "No Bones about It—Take #2," "This could go on forever. I could keep walking after the sound and essentially never get any closer to it. It's like playing a game. 'Look, I got the guy with the camera following me. He can't see me.'" Finally, he circled back around to his starting point, only to find a deer leg laid out beside the front tire.

He has also received gifts on the bicycle seat itself, the most impressive being a huge *tooth*.

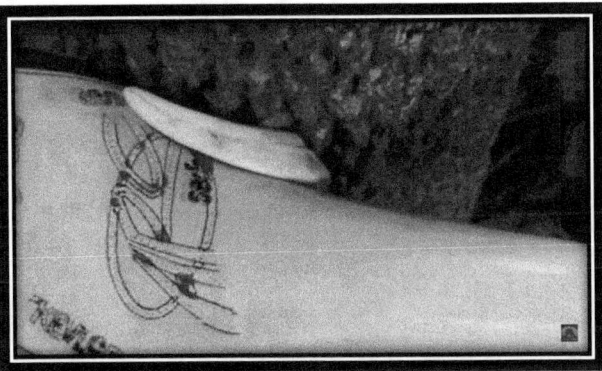

On another occasion, though, as he was riding back home, he was given something a bit less benign when a stone shot out of the trees and struck him directly in the mouth…hard.

The trail of blood is bright red in the video
"Sasquatch and the Flying Stone."

Yet, nothing can hold a candle to what Jim encountered on the afternoon of September 17, 2013. Hearing the sound of rocks being clacked together a couple hundred feet away, he walked in that direction. Suddenly, he was shocked and completely overwhelmed to see a chestnut-colored creature about seventy feet away, below him, making movements that exactly matched the rock clacking. With his video camera, Jim zoomed in; unfortunately, the subject was not facing him, but fortunately, she seemed entirely unaware of his presence. Fellow researchers will understand how vanishingly small are the chances of sneaking up on a Sasquatch before being wholly outsmarted and outflanked.

We may never fully understand why this episode falls so far outside the norm, but it is quite possible that the individual was simply distracted by three separate, simultaneous tasks.

The first was preparing food. After Jim knocked on a tree, the Sasquatch promptly stood and walked off, upright. When he descended to check her spot, he found two gray rocks scored with white impact abrasions, smashed acorns, apples, and several hairs left on the log she was just sitting on.

The second and third tasks that restricted her situational awareness were those of childcare, as I'll revisit in a moment.

These black-and-white stills do almost zero justice to the sharpness and drama of the high-resolution color footage, but I will print them here anyway to whet your appetite.

The sagittal crest is plainly visible.

Now check out the event itself in real-time HD: TimberGiantBigfoot's "Sasquatch - The Giant Revealed...Sept. 2013." After this, I'd recommend "Timbergiant 'A Giant Revealed' rock steady stabilization by M.K.Davis."

Then, the best analysis video of this footage is by ThinkerThunker: "TimberGiantBigfoot--New Discoveries!"   As you'll see, not only was the subject busy pounding nuts between two stones, but she was also preoccupied with an infant—whose little hand, gripping its mother's hair, can be seen flexing open and shut—and, it seems, another, older kid dashing about near her (evidence of whom appears in the opening sequence of this analysis video, though it is not identified as such in the analysis). What a perfect storm of maternal distraction!

Later, ThinkerThunker also points out that while Jim is inventorying the Sasquatch perch and unbeknownst to him, his camera briefly catches a large figure, probably the same individual, walking off through the trees.

Incidentally, near the end of Jim's footage, he films in passing a simple yet obvious structure right beside the Sasquatch's recent position—this in opposition to those who still argue that we can have no basis on which to attribute such formations to this species until the act of construction is directly documented. True, that will be a wonderful piece of video to behold one day soon, but the next best thing is a spatial/temporal association.

The same brand of skeptics are fond of trotting out the old distraction that since nobody has actually *witnessed* wood knocks being made, we cannot say who makes them. See "Sasquatch Tree Knocking Caught on Video for the First Time," which isolates one second of the "Mississippi Skunk Ape" clip.

8. Ogden, Utah—Population 87,000

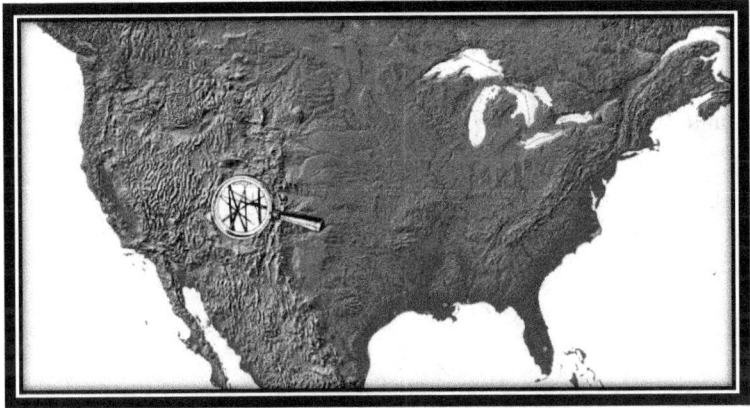

"Why is it so hard for people," asks Nathan Reo (Utah Sasquatch),

> to accept the idea that Sasquatch often live in greenbelts near urban areas? In Russia, wild dogs have learned to commute downtown using the subway system in the day, then at night they'll hop right back on the metro and head back out into the rural areas. Raccoons have urbanized to the extreme, even specializing their behaviors exclusively to eat garbage. Are we supposed to believe that a creature that looks, acts, and thinks like humans, with fewer differences than similarities, is incapable of living near urban areas?"

This researcher, though still relatively new on the scene, has already made significant contributions through his recognition of Sasquatch "terrain management"—how their tactics resemble those of Special Forces, masterfully employing cover-and-conceal techniques, fall-back positions, shadow and outline awareness, the "military crest" of ridges and mountainsides, etc. Also effective is his ability to clearly articulate the importance of structures and the method by which to locate them as well as numerous footprints. He has a firm grasp on the strange cultural and cognitive blind spots that keep mainstream society (not to mention science itself) from authentically perceiving what is right before our eyes.

For an exciting video of a late-night outing through the lens of a fellow researcher, exploring with Reo, see "Suburban Sasquatch! Wigwam, Whoops, Chatter, Structures Right in a Neighborhood" on the Sasquatch Omega YouTube channel.

I have put together a compilation of some of his best work as it relates to the topic of this book and called it "The Reo Reel: How Sasquatch and *Homo Sapiens* Territory Intersect." Here are some excerpts from his narration.

> What I've found down in the river bottoms in the city is just as impressive as, if not more than, all the stuff that I've found in the mountains. It is absolutely incredible how far these guys can come in and remain undetected.

> Near parking lots, if there's the brush and the undergrowth and the habitat, it always seems like they try to make a lookout, a place that's heavily, heavily concealed, guarded; no one's going to venture back here for any reason. From here, you can monitor the comings and goings of people because, in my opinion, Sasquatch are very concerned about what people are doing. We are clearly their greatest threat. It's important to constantly assess the threat. I think that it's their business, it's their full-time job to monitor humans, so they create these complex tunnels and hallways and channels through the trees. They tie the forest together, the bushes together. They put sticks everywhere so everything's blocked off, and it all becomes a gigantic maze that only they know.

A public park near Reo serves as an object lesson in how the parallel life of Sasquatch can remain undetected.

> This park is way more active than anybody knows.
> People contact me. Utahns know that I'm into
> Sasquatch, so everyone contacts me with their stories.
> And people aren't talking to each other about
> Sasquatch, and so everyone ends up being ignorant of
> their own neighbors. Everyone believes in Sasquatch
> and no one wants to admit it to each other, and so I end
> up getting all these stories that are happening currently.
> And they don't know that five other of their neighbors
> have contacted me as well, and I don't tell them
> because I respect people's wishes to be confidential.
>
> And so, in this neighborhood, tons of people have told
> me about this stuff, but everyone remains in ignorance
> about how active this park is. And Sasquatch actually
> *use* this ignorance as part of their repertoire! Half of
> the sightings that I'm getting from here are from
> people when they were younger, and they don't know
> that it's still happening. A lot of the people around here
> think that it was an older phenomenon, because
> generally people don't want to disclose things until
> thirty or forty years after the fact.

It's funny, the secrecy that surrounds Sasquatch, the shame, the *public* shame. People are so afraid of admitting that they believe in something that's culturally so frowned on, so taboo. Meanwhile, you have all these experiences that are happening, so they dump it onto me, and I end up with some really cohesive information.

From 15:43-33:50 of "The Reo Reel," he focuses on a small city, just one of the several he has kept close tabs on over the past two years.

I chose this particular community because it's so fascinating to me, the behaviors exhibited. I think it's representative of Sasquatch behavior in general. Okay, these green lines represent routes of travel. All of these little Bigfoot [icons] are places where I have personally gone and seen significant sign. These yellow markers are all sightings. I've either gotten these directly or they are from the grapevine, the Internet or otherwise. South Weber has a super-rich history of Sasquatch sightings…

He then proceeds to lay out this history graphically on the Google Earth satellite shot, breaking down the different greenbelts, micro forests, concealed corridors, their comparative attributes, and their associated level of recent activity—an anatomy of a human settlement veined through by Sasquatch pathways.

Dr. Jeff Meldrum says there are probably not even five thousand Sasquatch in North America, and I'm thinking, Well, then how am I seeing so much activity? How on Earth am I finding all of these signs in all of these areas if there are so few Sasquatch?

Now, I'm not suggesting that Sasquatch are everywhere here in this town. I think that there are just a few families and that they are making a lot of structures. Maybe there's a family or a clan per canyon. I don't know, but it definitely seems that there are more than Dr. Meldrum suggests.

I'll even go out at one in the morning into these mountains and there are wood knocks. How are there wood knocks and whistling? Why would there be a Sasquatch where I am? Why wouldn't it be chilling over there in that canyon instead? Why would it be exactly where I am? I just don't understand that, if there are so few of them. Again, they're not everywhere. They need specific conditions. But the population is grossly underestimated.

There are three more very illuminating videos that I'd like to draw your attention to.

"Bigfoot Dumpster Diver" drills into one specific instance of an often-reported Sasquatch behavior.

If you're like me, you've heard accounts over the years about Sasquatch opportunistically scavenging from Dumpsters but have found it nearly impossible to believe that these creatures, so wild, so dignified, and so perfectly adapted to their forest niche, would stoop to a lazy method more suited to raccoons, rodents, and bugs.

Furthermore, if they did, why wouldn't it be an absurdly simple matter to catch them in the act?

And yet, in this video, after visiting a rest stop with a history of such nighttime sightings, Reo and a fellow researcher bushwhack uphill through two hundred feet of dense and twisted growth until they break out into an open corridor filled with bones, strewn garbage—the Dumpsters' former contents—and, yes, stick and tree structures. Nowhere in this encampment do we see signs of human occupation—such as fire pits, mattresses, blankets, sleeping bags, dishes, toilet paper, water and alcohol bottles, beer cans, cigarette butts, etc.

The last two on the Reo must-watch list, for our purposes, are "Bigfoot by the River, Part 1" and "Bigfoot by the River, Part 2."

In the first part, exploring between a city river and train tracks, he explains the differences between human-built structures (such as hunting blinds) and Sasquatch structures. He then demonstrates how following subtle sign—such as tree leans and stick hangs—can lead to much more elaborate formations, even within city limits.

Bigfoot By The River, Part 1

In the second part, he continues nearby, pointing out a complex network of tactical blinds and structures on a river bottom easement surrounded by private property.

9. La Crescenta, California—Population 20,000

CBS 2's Andrea Fujii reporting from the scene

"There may be a mysterious beast lurking in the foothills of the San Gabriel Valley…"

On the afternoon of June 2, 2017, Jacob Gardiner was walking in the woods behind his local YMCA when he started feeling uncomfortable, as though he were being watched. He scanned with his cell phone but saw nothing. Later review of his video footage revealed an ape-like figure swinging in the tree branches above Jacob.

Several television outlets jumped on the story, defaulting to the "escaped exotic pet" explanation. And then, less than four miles from that site, researcher Angeles Sasquatch documented three structures and a large clump of feces. See my video "It's Fun to Stay at (or near) the Y...M...C...A!" and please check out Angeles Sasquatch's YouTube channel.

Here is the YMCA's location, tucked against the foothills.

When Angeles Sasquatch explored up behind the facility, he found human debris dispersed in a manner quite similar to what Nathan Reo documented in "Bigfoot Dumpster Diver"; that is, one would first think of homeless people and then realize what the site entirely lacks: fire pit, bedding logically set up, shelter, water bottles, alcohol bottles/cans, dishes, toilet paper, cigarette butts, drug paraphernalia. And yet, objects are consciously arranged.

A foam mattress oddly held onto a ledge by two branches. It would dry no more quickly up here than on the ground; see how thin it is.

CDs

The next step at this site will be to leave an audio recorder up there for an extended period.

La Crescenta lies between the Gabriel Mountains and the San Rafael Hills.

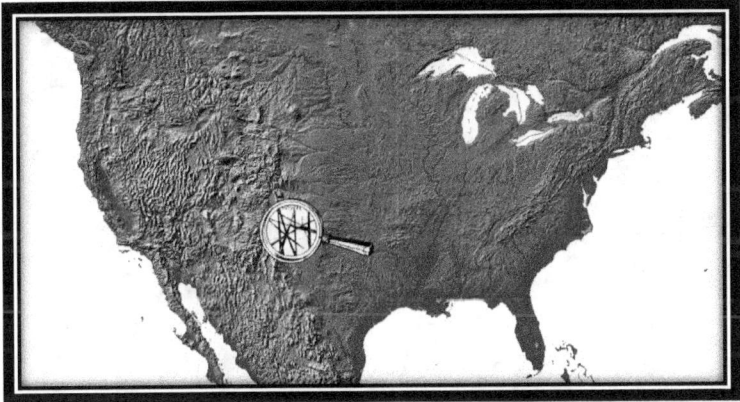

Such bleed-throughs from the realm of Sasquatch reality into mainstream media consciousness will only increase. In a breaking case out of New Mexico, forestry officials are concerned about numerous "mystery structures" appearing in the woods, some made up of "as many as a thousand pieces of wood"; see the video "'Mysterious Stick Structures' in New Mexico."

This one comes complete with the classic Sasquatch side show—miniature versions. (See *lateral corroboration*, p. 191 below.)

Notice the non-functional piling on of hundreds and hundreds of extra branches.

This t-pee is non-functional in the other direction—sparse and aesthetically pleasing but providing no meaningful shelter.

10. Barrie, Ontario—Population 190,000

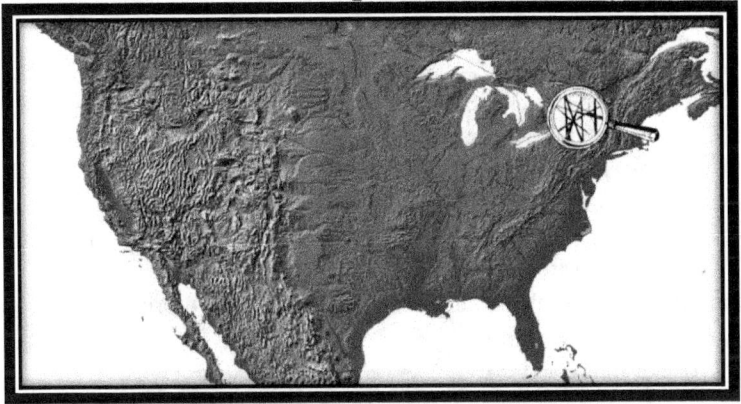

LeeAnn Carnegie (YouTube channel Southern Ontario Sasquatch Research) focuses on the forests south of Barrie on protected conservation land. Some of Canada's oldest known indigenous sites are located here, dating as far back as ten thousand years. She has found structures from the western end of Lake Erie to the eastern end of Lake Ontario, and as far north as Algonquin Park. Some of these forests are directly adjacent to private and public city properties; therefore, the habitat is scrupulously guarded against vandalism and degradation. Codes of conduct within these parks, ravines, and river corridors are often extremely strict: For instance, it is illegal to camp, make fires, or to "disturb, damage or destroy a plant, a part of a plant or any other naturally occurring object"; visitors are also forbidden to "harvest timber in the Park." (laws-lois.justice.gc.ca/eng/AnnualStatutes/2015).

And yet, these environments are rich with constructions that are constantly appearing, growing, and changing, sometimes from week to week; see "Sasquatch Rebuild! A New Stick Structure Built within Ten Days."

LeeAnn has shared with me a rich personal history.

I started discovering the possibility that Sasquatch are right here in the southern Ontario back in 1988. That is a long story, which happened to me as teenager, and I would be happy to share it at some point. Due to my age and vulnerability to social judgement, I repressed that experience for understandable reasons. It shook me to my core, but I did my best to keep it under wraps. That experience continued to surface over time…and I realize now that a measurable, tangible shift happened to me on that evening. Thankfully, I can understand the fear of what I experienced much better now as an adult and can talk about it from a more objective standpoint.

The clincher happened six summers ago. I was berry-picking close to our family cottage near Ottawa. I was by myself back in the woods, a large area of Crown Land, along an old lumber road that was overgrown from being used for harvesting timber several years previous. I'd been going in there for a few years to pick berries, as they grew along the old road. A little aside…I was an outdoor educator for many years in my teens and twenties and I know to always make lots of noise when walking back into the forest by myself. I know how healthy the black bear population is around our cottage, and I would never want to have an unexpected encounter. I was right in the middle of a tall mulberry bush. It was like a thick wall of vines,

and the berries were the size of my thumb knuckle. I'd
slowly and carefully weaseled my way in there,
avoiding the thorns as much as I could, so that I was
fully in the bush.

I'd been picking in there for a couple minutes, and all
of a sudden I heard a massive exhale, like a deep
guttural grrrruuuuuhhh! It was so clear and broad and
deep, and it's like it made the insides of my own body
resonate. I have no words to explain how that felt.
Massive deep vibration. And it was so similar to what I
had heard during my 1988 encounter. The guttural
exhale instantly shook me to my core. I looked, and I
saw what I now know was a juvenile Sasquatch step
out from the back of the bush and walk away into the
healthy, old, mixed forest. The entire berry bush shook
as it stepped away. I am not sure if it shook the
branches on purpose, or whether it was just the result
of the Sasquatch stepping out of the bush. I realized in
that moment it had to have been in there with me the
entire time I had been picking berries. I never saw or
smelled or heard anything. And I know for certain I
had been yelling and singing my entire way in along
the path. I was a young mother at the time, and the last
thing I wanted was to get into serious trouble with a
bear while berry picking for homemade jam.

I saw it walk away, I heard it walk away, I saw the deeply dark outline of its head and shoulders and body….and in that moment I felt such overwhelming fear. It was the most intense fight-or-flight moment I've ever had. I ran out of that bush. I dropped my berries, tore my way out of the bushes and I ran all the way back to the car, over a kilometre. I never looked back the entire way.

I was shaken for days. I went through so many levels of emotion…of denial, of thinking I was insane, fear of being judged if I spoke of it to anyone…and part of me beat myself up for putting myself in that situation in the first place. It was a very emotional experience, but I couldn't fully explain what all the feelings meant. All I knew my life had changed in that instant. I experienced a paradigm shift that was unforgettable. I had to talk myself into trusting my senses…trusting what I heard and seen and felt in that very moment. I knew I needed to find people who I could talk to, and who could offer me some form of guidance and support.

I finally reached out to an organization called Ontario Wildlife Field Research (OWFR). It is a safe place for eyewitnesses to report unique animal sightings, such as cougar and Sasquatch and other creatures, from around Ontario. I shared my experience with them through an email. A few key researchers, such as the founder of the OWFR, Peter Smith, believed me and my story, and that's when I kind of cracked open. Peter took me under his wing and took the time to listen and share his wisdom.

I became obsessed with the subject of Sasquatch and developed an unrelenting passion to learn and understand as much as I could. I remember that feeling so clearly. It was like a spiritual and emotional awakening. I couldn't get enough of the subject. I had never felt anything like this before.

I spent a lot of time learning over the next few years…reading and watching videos and connecting with people throughout Ontario. I was brought into the inner circle of the OWFR, where I was given access to private eyewitness reports that came into the site and that were not open to the general public. I did a bunch of interviews and site visits to meet with eyewitnesses and to check locations of sightings and prints. I documented their experiences for the OWFR. I met with honest people…hard-working men and women who were doing their best to balance daily life as a family member, neighbour and co-worker, and who were still processing their own paradigm shifts. Talking with them was like half documenting time and half support-group time. I was thrilled I could speak about my own experiences and it meant so much that I could see that there were others who could understand…who were processing similar encounters to those that I had had. I interviewed people and did site visits several hours away from my home around southern Ontario.

Reflecting on my own experiences and combining them with the many eyewitness accounts brought me to the conclusion that Sasquatch are indeed right here in southern Ontario. And they are not only in the vast forests where I had my berry picking encounter, they are throughout rural farmland, along rivers, in protected parklands, and on the outskirts of large urban centres.

The summer following my berry-picking incident, I began finding all kinds of stick structures in the woods near my cottage—stars and asterisks and high snaps and bends and leans. I remember sharing many of these discoveries with Peter Smith. His wisdom and guidance helped inspire me further, and it was that summer that I began picking up fourteen-to-sixteen-inch prints in wet leaves…exactly in the area I was finding stick formations. Also in early May of that year, I discovered a fourteen-inch, four-toed print on wet sand, the day after the water level had dropped enough to expose the sand. These prints were also observed by some family members. I was no longer alone in this experience.

Two and a half years ago, I began exploring protected forests and conservation areas near where I live, and I found several very complicated and odd stick structures. Hunting and camping are illegal in these areas, and I compared their design and complicated construction with other stick formations found by research friends. A very good friend of mine, Mike Paterson, told me that they look very similar to the structures he had found near the site of his first Sasquatch vocalization. It wasn't too long after that that we met on an early winter morning and he took me to see these structures. I was flabbergasted. They were just like the ones I was finding near my hometown.

It was after that excursion with Mike that I became obsessed with exploring as many rural parklands, rivers, and conservation areas as possible. I was spending many early mornings on weekends making my way to new park regions to explore for signs of Sasquatch with trail maps folded in my pocket. Every time I went out, I found structures.

I have had a few conversations with park employees and have asked them about the strange teepees and intricately arranged piles of sticks seen on my walk. None of them have been able to give me an answer as to who built them or why they are here. A few of them had apparently never noticed them, even though some are within sight of trails. I have read many park documents that clearly state that to "disturb, damage or destroy a plant or part of a plant or any other naturally occurring object" is illegal and a finable offence. Most of these places insist dogs be kept on leashes and that visitors remain on marked trails, due to the sensitivity of the habitat. It made me wonder if these employees truly did not know or whether they are in the know but are choosing to keep tight lipped about it.

Every structure I found was an exceptionally thrilling experience and still is to this day. And the more I found, the more I was inspired to find. I began to learn their styles of similarity…see the quirkiness in some construction designs and document fascinating elements of their building. I began to discover the vast array of styles, sizes, and shapes. I was also finding newly built structures at locations that had recently had none. I also started to observe subtle changes in some of the structures and documented how some of them were changing over time. Please see my "Evolution of a Sasquatch Structure" video.

I have also found several dozen large prints in and

around structure locations. Over the last year and a half, I have also been doing night-time audio recording at two structure locations. I have listened to hundreds of hours of audio and have been given a tremendous amount of what I believe to be Sasquatch activity. I have picked up clear, repeated wood knocks, whistles, hand claps, tongue clucks, bipedal footsteps, various animal and bird mimicry, loud vocal screams and yells, and deep groans and guttural exhales. You can hear some of these in my video "Late-Night Sasquatch Activity Captured on Audio."

I am truly honoured to be discovering these incredible creations. The joy, love, and sense of wonder and mystery they invoke is truly a gift. I celebrate the opportunity to play a small role in this collective journey of understanding, and I am grateful to be able to share my research with others and to compare our findings from different parts of the world.

The eleven structures shown in this section represent less than 5% of those LeeAnn has documented in her videos. Notice the clear parallels to others shown earlier in the book. There is a great explosion of theme and variation along every river she checks.

If you like the videos she and I recommended above—and who would not be drawn in by her enthusiasm and keen eye for detail?—you'll want to check out all her others.

PART 2

THE NATURE OF THE "BEAST"
WHO ARE THEY AND WHY CAN'T WE MEET THEM?

11. First of All, They are a Fellow Human Species

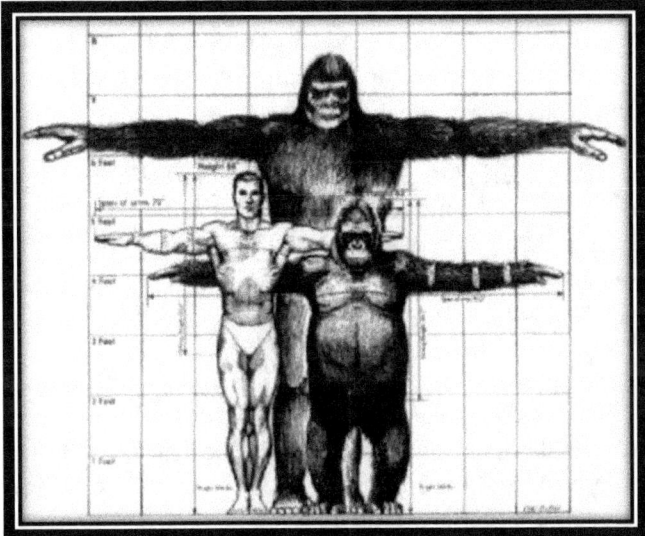

This section title may sound shocking, given how monstrous Sasquatch appear, but consider this: If we were to "correct" for just two traits—size and hair cover—would they look so different from us after all? Then, let's stand back further and ask, Why are thick hair and great stature necessarily non-human features anyway? They are not, of course. We know of tall, robust, and hairy people—just not quite so tall, robust, and hairy as our evolutionary next of kin. In terms of basic body morphology, when seen against the backdrop of the primate family tree, what our two species share far outweighs what we do not.

The most credible argument for Sasquatch humanity has been advanced by geneticist Melba Ketchum; see section 12 below. In the six years since the release of her historic study, detractors have continued to heap scorn upon her for daring to assert that this species is a human hybrid. And yet, science has marched steadily onward, affirming the credibility of her underlying assumption. Further breakthroughs in the sequencing of ancient DNA have only served to shore up the case for hybridization in human evolution generally; our *Homo* genealogy is, it turns out, riddled with it…or should I say *made possible by it*? Here are several among numerous sources to check out.

- "The Hybrid Origin of 'Modern' Humans": "Recent genomic research has shown that hybridization between substantially diverged lineages is the rule, not the exception, in human evolution." (*Evolutionary Biology*: 10/2015)

- "Human Evolution was Shaped by Interbreeding": "Our distant ancestors interbred with the Neanderthals and other hominin species. These hybridization events may have been crucial to our evolution." (BBC.com: 10/2015) [Note: The term *hominin* refers to members of the genus *Homo*, including, most recently, the Neanderthals, the Denisovans, *Homo floresiensis*, and *Homo sapiens*.]

- "Meet our Hybrid Ancestors who kept Extinct Humans' DNA Alive": Neanderthals, Denisovans, and other extinct humans live on inside our cells – but what was life like for the hybrid humans who carried their genes?" (newscientist.com: 4/2016)

An animal's hybrid pedigree can often be identified by the naked eye, as in the horse-zebra and lion-tiger crosses below. In each case, the parents are of different species but the same genus (*Equus* and *Panthera*).

Beyond the fact that countless eyewitnesses over the centuries have described Sasquatch as "like a cross between a gorilla and a person," here are three specific areas in which we can see a blending of human and non-human primate traits in the species.

1. Body Ratios

Though he does not mention Ketchum's contribution in "Cracking the Bigfoot Code," ThinkerThunker nonetheless presents clear supporting evidence. As you will see in the video, by comparing arm-to-leg ratios in humans, great apes, and Sasquatch, he finds that the Sasquatch ratio falls almost perfectly in between those of the other two primate types. *Homo sapiens* arms are much shorter than our legs; great ape arms are much longer than their legs; and Sasquatch arms are only a little bit shorter than their legs.

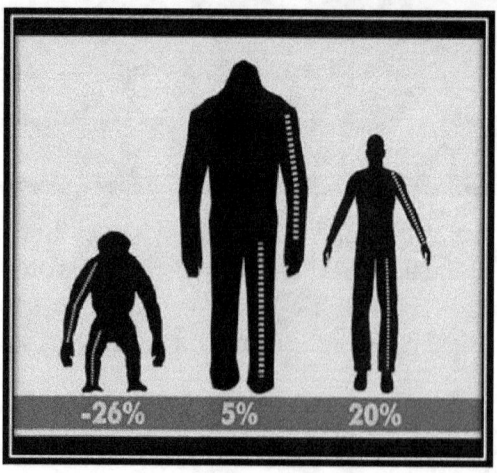

2. Foot Morphology

The great apes have an abducted big toe, which means it is separated from the other four toes, as seen below. We humans have an adducted big toe, joining the others at the front of the foot. Sasquatch have toes very much like ours in terms of position (though they are much longer and more flexible, like those of the great apes).

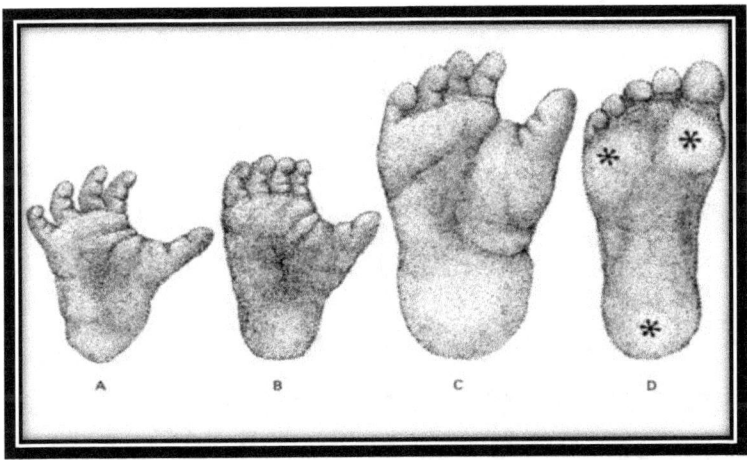

A=chimpanzee B=lowland gorilla C=mountain gorilla D=human

And yet, in another respect, Sasquatch feet are strikingly different from ours and much more like those of the great apes. Theirs lack the rigid, longitudinal arch that we possess; instead, their feet can flex in the middle by means of a *midtarsal break* or *hinge*, like those of the gorilla and chimpanzee.

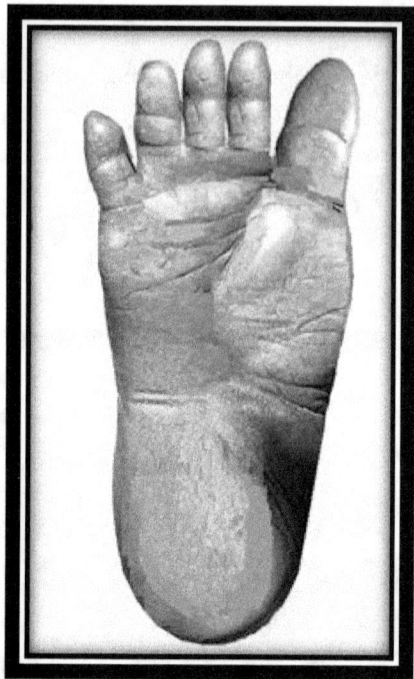

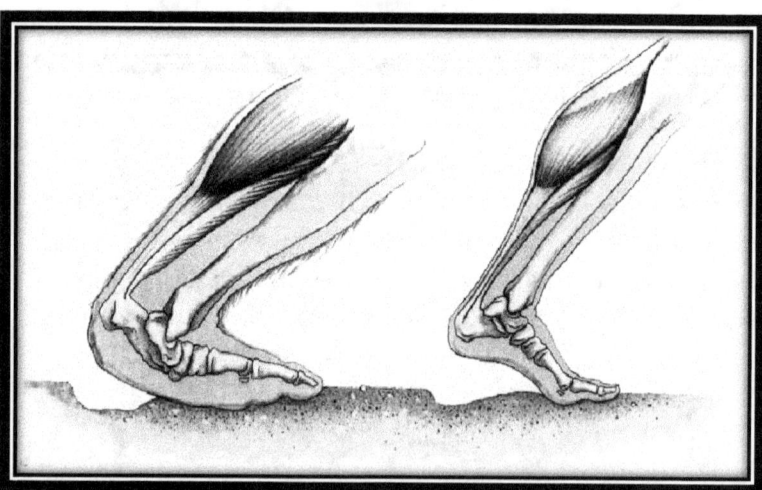

Dr. Jeffrey Meldrum's educated guess at the bone structure of the Sasquatch foot as compared to the human foot, based upon hundreds of Sasquatch track casts from across North America.

3. *From the Shoulders Up*

Sasquatch heads are proportionally much larger than ours and set down much lower between their shoulders, like those of the gorilla and the chimpanzee. They appear to have a sagittal crest, also like the gorilla. Their heavy brow ridge resembles that of the great apes and of the Neanderthal. Lastly, their jaws are proportionally more robust than ours, again like the great apes and the Neanderthal.

An artist's rendering of the Neanderthal, based upon skull morphology.

However, take a look at Patty's nose. It is "hooded" like ours, like the Neanderthal's, and like other members of the genus *Homo*, whereas the great apes' noses lack the hood.

Patty's remains the best facial shot available. Virtually every eyewitness who has gotten a good look has described the same human type of nose.

Orangutan and gorilla noses (chimps' are similarly forward facing)

12. Does the DNA Agree?

Yes.

This blending of physical characteristics, in Sasquatch, between those of *Homo sapiens* and those of non-human primates makes perfect sense in light of Melba Ketchum's landmark genetic study, "Novel North American Hominins, Next Generation Sequencing of Three Whole Genomes and Associated Studies," which was released on February 13, 2013.

You may have heard skeptics denigrating Ketchum's work; most scientific breakthroughs are initially rejected, of course, due to the ponderous conservatism of science itself. It hasn't helped that the study involved mostly Texas-based laboratories and researchers (there is an anti-south bias in mainstream consciousness) or that Ketchum herself, besides being a southerner, is also a woman, a blonde, a Christian, and a forensic geneticist with a doctorate in Veterinary Sciences rather than a traditional PhD. Academia disdains non-PhDs, no matter what they may bring to the table.

I'd recommend simply reading the study itself; you can download it at sasquatchgenomeproject.org. If you're a non-scientist like me, much of it will sail over your head, but you will get the gist. The headline from the study is that Sasquatch was originally produced as a hybrid between human females and males of another primate species, not yet discovered.

Here are Ketchum's co-authors.

- Patrick W. Wojtkiewicz—North Louisiana Criminalistics Laboratory, Shreveport, LA
- Aliece B. Watts—Integrated Forensic Laboratories, Inc., Euless, TX
- David W. Spence—Southwestern Institute of Forensic Sciences, Dallas, TX
- Andreas K. Holzenburg—Texas A&M University, Microscopy & Imaging Center, Department of Biology and Department of Biochemistry & Biophysics, College Station, TX
- Douglas G. Toler—Huguley Pathology Consultants, P.A., Ft. Worth, TX
- Thomas M. Prychitko—Helix Biological Laboratory, Detroit, Michigan
- Fan Zhang—UNT Center for Human Identification, University of North Texas Health Science Center, Fort, Worth, TX

Here are the laboratories that participated in the study, though they were not told what species they were looking at; thus, they were "blind" labs.

- Family Tree DNA Genomics Research Center, 1445 North Loop West, Suite 820, Houston, TX
- SeqWright, Inc., 2575 W. Bellfort St. Suite 2001, Houston, TX
- UT Southwestern Medical Center, 6000 Harry Hines Blvd. NA7.116, Dallas, TX
- USC Norris Comprehensive Cancer Center, 1441 Eastlake Avenue, Los Angeles, CA 90033
- Texas A&M University, Microscopy & Imaging Center, Department of Biology and Department of Biochemistry & Biophysics, College Station, TX
- Texas Veterinary Medical Diagnostic Laboratory, College of Veterinary Medicine, Texas A&M University, College Station, Texas

- Southwestern Institute of Forensic Sciences, 2355 North Stemmons Freeway, Dallas, TX

And here are the first two sentences of the study's abstract (summary).

One hundred and eleven samples of blood, tissue, hair, and other types of specimens were studied, characterized and hypothesized to be obtained from elusive hominins in North America commonly referred to as Sasquatch. DNA was extracted and purified from a subset of these samples that survived rigorous screening for wildlife species identification.

Before we proceed, a little context. There are two types of DNA in each animal cell, nuclear DNA and mitochondrial DNA. The former is found in the cell's nucleus and encodes the entire history of both maternal and paternal genetic contributions back through time. Outside the nucleus, but still within the cell, are mitochondria, tiny structures often called "the powerhouse of the cell" because they produce energy that cells need. Each mitochondrion—there are about 1,700 in every human cell—includes an identical loop of DNA (called mitochondrial DNA or mtDNA) that is about 16,000 base pairs long. (A base pair is the smallest unit of genetic information.)

In other words, mtDNA is much easier to isolate (within, say, a Sasquatch blood, tissue, or hair sample) and to analyze because there are so many more copies per cell and because each copy is so far simpler than the double helix system within the nucleus, which contains three billion base pairs.

And crucially—for purposes of species classification in the case of Sasquatch—mtDNA loops are passed down only from mother to offspring and therefore serve as portals into deep maternal antiquity. Continuing with the Ketchum study's abstract…

Mitochondrial DNA (mtDNA) sequencing…was conducted on purported Sasquatch DNA samples gathered from various locations in North America.

How were these one hundred and eleven samples gathered? I'll give just a couple of examples here; you can find more in Chapter Seven of the book *Sasquatch Rising 2013*.

New Mexico: JC Johnson (Blood Samples)

In 2010, researcher JC Johnson investigated a strange incident in which an eight-inch PVC pipe had sustained two punch holes; nearby lay the body of a skunk with its scent glands removed. Johnson and others pieced together what must have occurred and obtained samples from the copious blood found on the pipe. On JC Johnson's YouTube channel, see the video "The Harvest," and for further images of what the researchers found at the scene, see his "Skunk Attack Photos (night before)."

Johnson speculates on why it may be that the scent glands were harvested.

> With all the young Sasquatch that have been sighted in
> this area this year...[I thought that] if I had a youngster
> I wanted to hide and all the animals would leave it
> alone, the predators, the dogs, the coyotes, whatever, I
> would take skunk scent and put it all over my

youngster, and everything would leave it alone. A skunk lays by the side of a road until he evaporates. Ravens won't touch it, buzzards won't touch it. So, skunk's a good mask to hide behind.

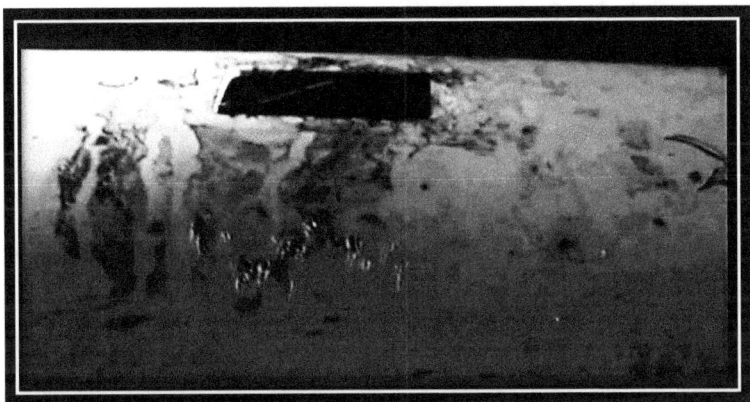

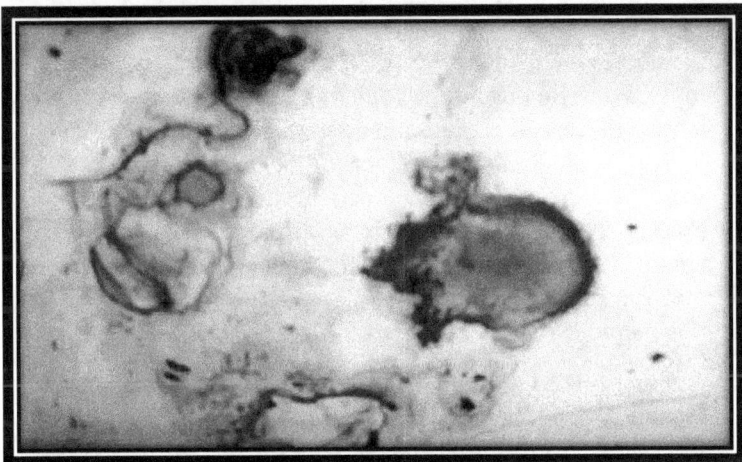

In breaking through the PVC pipe, the Sasquatch evidently cut its hands, leaving blood on the outside, which was then included in the Ketchum study.

Tennessee: Scott Carpenter (Hair Samples)

Scott Carpenter is a researcher in Eastern Tennessee who has had great success, born of persistence and ingenuity, in making contact and gathering hair samples. He speaks about his methods on the November 25th, 2012, episode of "Bigfoot Tonight," hosted by Chuck Prahl and Stacy Hostetler.

I baited a tree. There were three different methods I used. The first big sample I collected I actually just put [the tape] on the tree, because I had a trail camera and a few weeks before I'd gotten a video where they were hiding behind this tree and peeking out at the camera. So I said, "Aha. I know where you guys are spying my camera." So I went in there with the packing tape and went around that tree backwards, sticky side out. Then I went back in a couple weeks later to check the SD cards, and that's when the tape was torn off the tree and laying on the ground with this huge amount of four-to-six-inch black hair in it, just a huge amount. And so that was my first sample.

And then, I was trying to figure out a way to lure them in, and that's when we came up with the bacon grease. We were looking for something to put on the tree that would get them against it. And I already knew they love bacon. So during the colder part of the weather I would smear bacon grease in the   bark of a tree, as high as I could reach, nine foot off the ground. And then I would wrap packing tape at three different levels. Periodically, they'd come by and lean up against the tree and lick the bacon grease and happily give me some hair samples. I didn't get as much with this method. I'd get a dozen or so hairs, but it did work.

Another thing I did like this was, I'd place apples up in the notch of a tree and then I'd wrap tape, and I'd get a few hairs   off of their hands or underneath their arms when they'd reach to get the apple out of the tree.

And then the [last] method I used I just stumbled on by seeing what would happen in nature. I noticed going into one of my areas there had been a holly bush that had broke off, and when it broke off it made like a cone…the splinters…it had actually caught some hair. So I collected that hair and got the idea. I went along this trail, with gloves on, broke some trees off of my own, forming that natural hair-catch. And I actually got about a dozen strands of hair doing that.

So during a two-year period, I collected quite a bit. The low-tech methods work best. I'm sure a lot of scientists out there   are going to be swallowing their tongues, seeing that some guy *from the South* has gotten good evidence with bacon grease and packing tape.

Also, stringing black sewing thread between trees at seven foot has been a good indicator of whether the Bigfoot are moving through an area or not. That has told me where to put my tape traps [and] my trail cameras.

I had an area that they walked through pretty common and I put the black thread up between two trees, and he broke it three weeks in a row, then all of a sudden he stopped breaking it. But I could see by the ground clutter that he was still moving through, so obviously he'd gotten used to it...Oh, the idiot's putting thread. So I did this 360 around the trail, and sure enough I went back a week later and he'd gone two trees over and tried to go between two other trees. And I'd just love to have been a fly on the wall when he broke *that* thread. That's just a little bit of satisfaction, aggravating them as much as they aggravate me. I think they've got a sense of humor and enjoy screwing with us, so it was nice to pull one over on them.

Low-tech methods like that. In low parts of the trail actually laying a stick on the ground, and seeing if it gets kicked, that sort of thing has worked as well. Or they'll step on it and break it. Little things, that's been my bread and butter.

Carpenter places a "tape trap"; see the fascinating how-to video "Hair Samples - Bigfoot DNA Collection -BCBFRP-Update-1-14-2012"

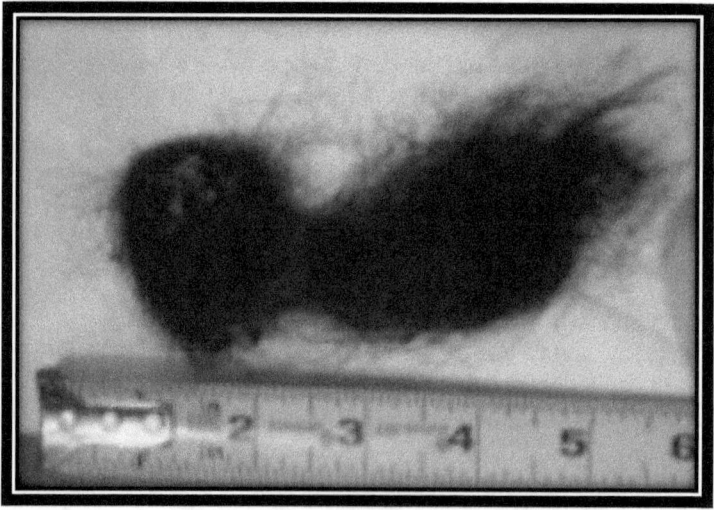

Now let's finish with Ketchum;s abstract. The term *haplotypes*, below, refers to the historical distribution of human groups across the earth; our mtDNA can tell us where our ancestors came from, which is what people pay for in services such as 23andMe.

The mtDNA haplotypes obtained were uniformly
consistent with modern humans. Of the 20 whole and 10
partial mitochondrial genomes sequenced, 16 diverse
haplotypes were found, suggesting that these hominins
did not originate in a single geographic location.

Three of the Sasquatch samples were subjected to next
generation whole genome sequencing, each of which
independently yielded high quality complete genomes.
The totality of the DNA evidence suggests the
Sasquatch nuclear DNA is a mosaic comprising human
DNA interspersed with sequences that are novel but
primate in origin. (SasquatchGenomeProject.org)

In other words, what Ketchum found is that Sasquatch mtDNA
is virtually identical to that of modern human mtDNA, whereas
Sasquatch nuclear DNA contains primate DNA and other,
unrecognizable sequences. (Since we now have the whole
Neanderthal and Denisovan genomes, Ketchum has been able to
rule out those extinct human cousins as the potential male
progenitor of the Sasquatch line.)

In an interview with Ed Brown of bigfoottruth.blogspot.com,
she presents the case clearly. It's important to note that when she
says "modern human," she means *anatomically* modern; she places
the likely era of hybridization in the range of fifteen thousand years
ago.

The mtDNA of Sasquatch is 100% modern human, and
we were not the first to get those results. Four university
labs, testing some of the same samples, had identical
sequences to our results. Since species ID is done with
mtDNA, this clearly establishes their humanity. The
nuDNA nuclear DNA is a mixture of human sequence
and a novel sequence. The novel sequence has never
been seen so we do not know what it comes from.

Many shudder and recoil from the very notion of a human
hybrid, though as mentioned above, advances in the sequencing of
ancient DNA continue to reveal, at a rapid pace, our own mixed-

species heritage. For those hobbled by an egocentric belief in human exceptionalism—in which the term *human* has room for only one species—it will be a painful leap indeed to sincerely entertain the proposition that not only is Sasquatch somehow "related to humans" but, moreover, that when they originally appeared on Earth, they were no less than *half* human, and that today, though much farther removed from us genetically (because they've reproduced with their own kind for a thousand generations), they remain a fellow member of the genus *Homo* and therefore our zoological next of kin.

So deep-seated is this resistance that every time a new Sasquatch hair sample—far too thick and coarse to be one of ours, its tips tapering rather than cut—yields human mtDNA, we hear a reflexive chorus of "contamination" claims; the researchers *must* have accidentally mixed in their own DNA. As a long-time forensic geneticist who has testified as an expert witness in court, Ketchum knows full well how to wash samples prior to testing; see her video "How We Proved There Was No Contamination in the Sasquatch Genome Project Samples."

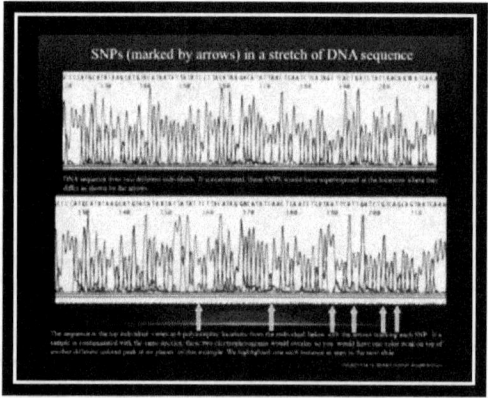

An important corroborating example of an organic sample that has been falsely dismissed as contaminated is that of the Orang Pendek, or "short man," a Sumatran version of Sasquatch that stands just three to five feet tall. When a hair sample was submitted to world-renowned geneticist Thomas Gilbert at the Centre for GeoGenetics at the Natural History Museum of Denmark, he ran the mtDNA sequence, and the results came back "human." Meanwhile, a morphological analysis of the sample showed definitively that the hair structure was far from human. This is the very same yawning disconnect that Ketchum has turned up between genetic and visual identification, revealing that the category "human" needs immediate corrective expansion. See her video "Support of Sasquatch Genome Project Results by another Scientist."

On her Facebook page, she has written that

> After reading the new *Nature* article about humans cross-breeding with other [ancient] hominins, I just can't understand why there is such an aversion to our study. Our findings are just like those that find humans with a percentage of Neanderthal DNA, only ours show the novel Sasquatch DNA to be predominant in the genomes, with the human component being the lesser contributor. In other words, Sasquatch are Sasquatch, with a little *Homo sapiens* remaining in them from the original crossbreeding long ago. It is really simple to understand.

13. If They're Human, Why do They Act so Cold and Distant?

Well, "cold and distant" are in the eye of the beholder. Evasion or withdrawal do not necessarily mean rejection or even disinterest. Someone who sneaks around to achieve the most protected vantage point on a subject may care deeply about that subject, care enough to demand privacy for maximum observational richness.

By the same token, however—on the flip side—Sasquatch do not exclusively steer clear of us; they also approach us, though in a very peculiar way. They come in at an oblique angle, especially at so-called *habituation sites*. These are places where our two species become slightly more conversant with each other than usual, mutually familiarized, where Sasquatch seem to feel at liberty to exercise an innate curiosity toward us and an impulse to interact.

What they do *not* do, even here, is to emerge into the open for easy viewing and videotaping; daylight sightings at habituation sites are as rare as daylight sightings generally. What they *do* do here is to peek out from behind trees at a distance, at night, occasionally visible in the moonlight, swaying back and forth or just standing stock still, watching the house. Add to this a typical suite of overtures, played out repeatedly and consistently at residences across North America.

- Slapping or banging on the walls of the house, outbuildings, or vehicles
- Window peeking
- Window tapping/screen scraping
- Leaving "gifts" (feathers, pretty stones, dead animals, animal parts, etc.) or human objects (dolls, tools, jewelry, etc.) that the residents have never seen before
- Throwing projectiles at residents from out of sight during the daytime (pebbles, stones, sticks, limbs, pine cones, clumps of dirt, etc.)
- Throwing projectiles at the walls, windows, or onto the roof at night
- Removing toys, tools, or other items from the yard/porch/garage/vehicles/outbuildings
- "Borrowing" items and returning them later
- Manipulating/arranging/rearranging of objects
- Stone clacking
- Subtle snapping of sticks and branches (as researcher Kelly Shaw puts it, "Sasquatch have a snapping habit")
- Wood knocks/taps/limb breaks/violent tree pushes from nearby in the woods

- "Spying" on children in broad daylight,
  especially while they are at play (e.g.,
  swimming, jumping on a trampoline, etc.);
  the children themselves will catch glimpses,
  not the adults
- Vocals (howls, whoops, moans, yelps, mimicry
  of animals, machines, and people)
- Spoken language, variously described as
  "chatter" sounding Russian, Asian, or like
  human speech being rapidly played backward
- Muffled but palpable thumps on the ground, felt
  as vibration in one's chest
- Stick and tree structures appearing in the yard or
  nearby woods
- Sudden bodily sensations as from an electric
  shock, often referred to as being "zapped"
  and resulting in disorientation, weakness,
  nausea, vertigo, paralysis, fear, dread or,
  occasionally, pleasure/well-being
- Unexplained lights in the woods/"orbs" in motion

Some people, when faced with such unnerving breaches of ordinary reality, recoil in alarm and anxiety; one friend of mine described herself as feeling constantly "under siege." Others embrace the experience as a great adventure. Both ends of the spectrum are represented in this book, which contains vivid, first-person testimonials from six families spread across North America.

Most of those who welcome the opportunity to connect with these kindred visitors find success only once they learn how to adapt to the Sasquatch's singular style of interaction. They harness their penchant for gift-giving and for arrangement/rearrangement of objects in order to play games of indirect—or mediated—communication.

In Part 3, below, I will flesh out, with many examples, what is possible within the contours of this unique relationship.

14. How Do They All Learn the Exact Same Behavior?

They don't, any more than birds learn how to make a nest.

During the past five decades—since the Patterson/Gimlin Film—in which Sasquatch research has been seriously pursued both in this country and worldwide, the most salient characteristic of the species, their unparalleled elusiveness, has been consistently understood within the framework of learning and conscious choice. Matthew Moneymaker, for instance, speculates that "They've seen human activity that seemed endearing or sympathetic. You've probably watched people having fun somewhere, from a distance. And you wish you could go and have fun with them too. I think they watch us and probably plenty of times they wish they could just freely walk among us. But they *know* they can't."

This cannot be the whole, or even the primary, explanation. The very notion of generational transmission of knowledge—children learning the ropes from their elders—necessarily entails variability in educational success. For many reasons, not all family groups or clans would be equally proficient at imparting threshold savvy to the young; keep in mind the many imperfections and oversights of instruction, relating to quality of instructor and aptitude of pupil.

In order to maintain, day after day, century after century, and throughout the entire planet, an avoidance track record so close to 100% that we still lack absolute proof, they cannot afford even one fatal lapse. One.

That level of infallibility is simply not plausible within the proposed category of a learned skill set. It would be as if birds had to depend upon parental training in order to master nest-building

...and not only that, but also as if a single failure meant something irrevocably tragic for the fate of all birds everywhere.

We need a much tighter form of explanation, one that matches the necessarily restricted, manageable scope of Sasquatch choice. While most eye-witness encounters do indeed seem to arise from momentary Sasquatch "mistakes"—such as being taken by surprise while distracted (like "Patty," whose eighteen seconds of well-filmed exposure nearly blew the whole operation), not hiding quite well enough, or letting curiosity get the better of them—these never extend to any wholesale decision to drop their defenses and "freely walk among us." Not even close. Small-scale errors fall within the narrow range of variation to be expected of any inherited behavior profile, errors including brief inattention or slips of judgment, but not including the ultimate, irreversible mistake that would imperil the entire species.

Since it defies logic to presume that adults could remain virtually flawless, in this broad sense, over decades of life, consider the premise that the children, too, would have to avoid disaster even when still in their wayward years, too young to have fully internalized the lessons. Within the grand contest of evasion, not only would the array of finer tactical points take years to perfect, if it were not hardwired from birth, but the foundational principle itself—STAY AWAY FROM THE HUMANS—would certainly be violated on some occasions, here and there, now and then.

Well, let me amend that. It's true that juvenile Sasquatch have indeed been reported to approach juvenile *Homo sapiens*, resulting in unforgettable face-to-face encounters, but they always end up walking or running off; thus, the episodes conclude with the foundational principle being restored, no permanent harm done. While the *sapiens* girl or boy, overwhelmed and amazed, often wishes the "hairy kid" would stay around and play, the visitor never does, never tosses aside the bedrock ground rule. Uniformly, given the two options, Sasquatch young and old "select" distance, not consciously, not because it has been drilled into them or because they have been persuaded of the merits of the choice, but because distance is in their core nature, in their bones—steadily maintained or quickly reestablished after every (rare) lapse.

Therefore, their constellation of faculties and impulses must be a very compact one, unyielding, allowing for almost no wiggle room, variation, or meaningful freedom of choice. That is, their limitations are as key to their survival as are their capacities. Otherwise, we simply would not find Sasquatch still existing— indeed, thriving—as they do today.

In my view, the secret to their success lies in the way this species *thinks*. It is this that sets it apart from us most dramatically and allows it—constantly, automatically—to baffle our own thought processes.

Once we accept the reality that Sasquatch are a fellow human species and situate their main advantages on the cognitive plane, our natural tendency is then to construe their mind on the model of the *Homo sapiens* mind and to ask, How could *we* accomplish what they accomplish in the forest?

The answer is that we could not. Or, more accurately, the *typical* human being plainly lacks the strategic genius and sheer mental processing power to replicate Sasquatch feats. If this species is governed, then, by ancient hardwiring, how might this profile best be understood? Is there an explanatory resource already on the table, perhaps, a theoretical framework, some broader context in which their breathtaking exploits might find a place within a known psychological category?

15. Another Layer of Kinship

> Autism is not a bright, shiny key. It is more like the
> rusted, scratched, and twisted thing one finds discarded
> in the dust, but as we all must surely remember from
> our childhood tales, it is precisely that type of key—the
> one most likely to be overlooked—that in the end
> succeeds in opening an essential door. (Alan Griswold,
> *Autistic Symphony*)

Many wild animals are adept at eluding human detection, but they don't also pivot *toward* us. As far as I'm aware, only two creatures on Earth fit this double-sided behavioral profile:

- Avoid *direct* contact with human beings
- Seek *indirect* contact with human beings

The two are Sasquatch and autistic people.

Of course, I am not proposing that Sasquatch "have autism" in any reductively clinical sense; that would be foolish, given the preliminary state of our knowledge. What I have noticed, however, is a strikingly similar cluster of traits and gifts that we may take up, experimentally, as a framework through which to get a handle of Sasquatch nature and behavior.

Autism has ancient roots; we can find examples of the syndrome way back through history—see *Not Even Wrong: A Father's Journey into the Lost History of Autism*, by Paul Collins—so it's not just some modern-day aberration. Also, it's highly heritable on the small scale of families and could therefore plausibly run in an entire species. Gorillas, for instance, share many traits with people "on the spectrum"; see *Songs of the Gorilla Nation*, by Dawn Prince-Hughes. Increasingly, geneticists are pinpointing the genes that underlie this constellation of traits; see, for instance, the article "DNA Scan Uncovers 18 Genes Newly Associated with Autism" at NBC.com.

My hunch is that Sasquatch and autistic people probably do share a lot of these same genes and the resultant brain circuitry, inherited from a common ancestor, but that this endowment has taken different paths in our two cases down through time so that today the strong parallels are supplemented by certain contrasts. The main contrast is Sasquatch's obvious ability to work together like a well-oiled machine. Unlike human autistics, they do not isolate as individuals. For human autistics, it seems that all people are the Other, whereas for Sasquatch, fellow members of their own kind seem to be extensions of the self, leaving only our own species as the Other.

Some have attacked my theory as though I am claiming that Sasquatch are "mentally ill" or afflicted with a "disorder." On the contrary, the particular variety of autism that most closely parallels Sasquatch abilities is that of the autistic *savant*. These are cognitively gifted individuals who, though socially isolated, score at a genius level when it comes to visual intelligence (e.g., eidetic, or photographic, memory) and the processing of information.

Autistic savant chess grandmaster David Navara

For an overview of my Sasquatch Savant Theory, see the video "The Mind of Sasquatch and the Secret to their Success," or you can read the full treatment in the book *The Sasquatch Savant Theory*.

Generally speaking, those on the moderate to severe end of the spectrum strive to keep themselves at a safe remove from others at all costs, existing, as the phrase goes, "in their own world." They don't stay physically apart from humanity, hidden away like Sasquatch, but they do stay inwardly so, protecting a profoundly vulnerable interior life. Any frontal exposure of this true self feels disastrous.

In Donna Williams's groundbreaking study, *Exposure Anxiety—The Invisible Cage: An Exploration of Self-Protective Responses in the Autism Spectrum and Beyond*, she presents a rich and nuanced treatment of this condition. For our purposes, I will brazenly apply her "and Beyond" to Sasquatch and propose that the mainspring beneath their relentlessly evasive maneuvers must be a powerful version of this very same anxiety.

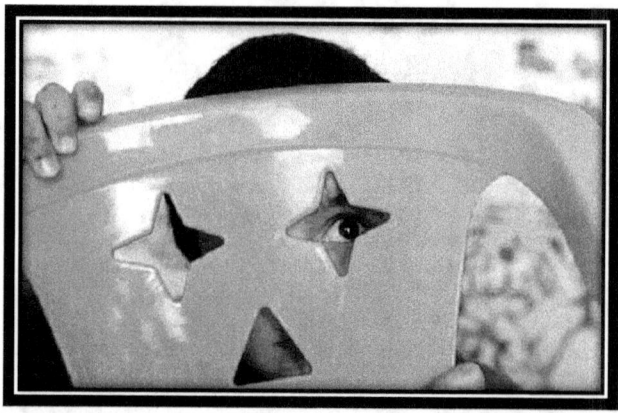

Autistic people do, however, overcome this resistance at times and communicate with people—like Sasquatch at habituation sites—when they can do so without compromising their sense of security and stability, which is to say indirectly.

For twenty years, my friend Michael worked with autistic adults at a group home in Alaska. He shared with me many instances in which he'd use objects to mediate social contact with them. One of his clients used to leave him "treasures," simple surprises hidden in a drawer or a cupboard. As soon as Michael would arrive at work, he would locate that day's surprise. "I had to find it, because that was the opening...so that we could interact." Another client responded best to a stuffed bear; he and Michael would routinely play a game of hide and seek with it.

> The bear was a gateway to him. It was a road that
> was clear of doubt on his part because the few who

knew how to interact with the bear and travel this
road were safe people

Success can be found through more officially therapeutic
methods as well, such as the Picture Exchange Communication
System (or PECS).

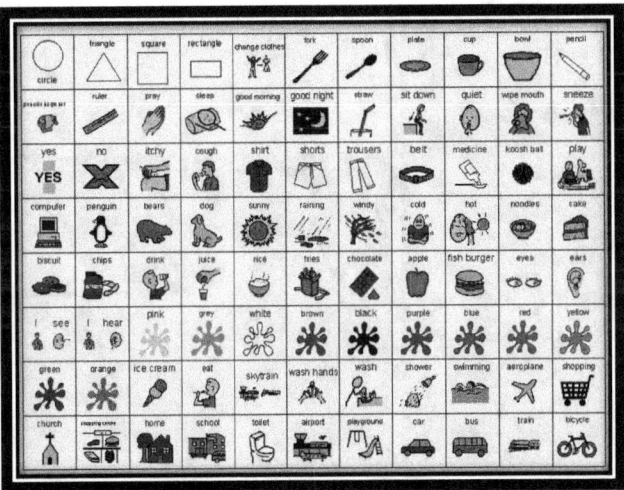

A typical array of PECS cards.

These cards can facilitate communication.

Sometimes, autistic people use objects not to communicate but rather to shore up their own realms, to solidify their ground, to create order and control within a world that often feels overwhelmingly chaotic and threatening; control is an ultimate concern.

Common autistic stacking and aligning behavior

Creating a structured safety or "buffer" zone.

Many find solace in working with machines (physical) or information (intellectual), both of which can ground them emotionally. Dawn Prince-Hughes, author of *Songs of the Gorilla Nation*, writes of her childhood that

> I gained some relief by arranging things. Most autistic people need order and ritual and will find ways to make order where they feel chaos. Things were made to fit together in ways that always made sense, in never-failing patterns that had purpose.
>
> Machines were both reliable and aesthetic. I had a very developed aesthetic sense and was constantly framing the world around me with borders informed by purpose and balance.

16. A Few Further Affinities

© 2014 DAVID A. CLAERR

Many of the following connections are drawn using examples of autistic children, but of course I do not mean to infantilize our close cousins; if anything, in many ways, compared to us, *they* are the adults. The sad fact is, though, that much more information is available about young folks on the spectrum than about adults, because once grown up, they usually fall out of the clinical system; social services are geared toward the early years.

Stimming/Self-Soothing through Rhythmic Percussion

Autistic people tend, when anxious, to engage in behaviors that calm and stabilize them, restoring equilibrium. This is called *stimming*. They will drum their fingers, flap their hands, and fiddle with objects "to release excess energy." In *Exposure Anxiety*, Donna Williams writes that "Rhythm is one way of shifting perception. If things seem too in your face, a rhythm can make them more external...[providing] a framework to make them digestible. It is about building a safe space, a foundation."

My video "Morning Visits 2014: Daily Interactions with a Sasquatch Group" contains hundreds of instances of drumming in the forest by an individual I came to call Music Man. I have since learned of other researchers who have documented the same behavior, Sasquatch percussion that does not seem solely meant for communication; see "The Sasquatch Savant Theory 4: Why Do They Drum?"

In the group home, my friend Michael worked with a young man who wore a drum on a strap around his neck.

> The drum was part repetitive behavior and part a zone to go into, a mantra. He constantly beat out a rhythm with his thumb that didn't change. It brought some kind of safety to him. It was a safety sound, a bubble of sound that eased his anxiety. It was a sign of contentment sometimes too. Other times, a sign of distress. You could kind of tell [the difference] because the pattern would change a little bit.

Stimming/Self-Soothing through Swaying and Rocking

This autistic trait is very familiar. Reports of Sasquatch swaying and rocking, too, are quite common. You can actually watch one doing so in the video "Clips from the Michael Greene Thermal Footage." When I visited a family in New Hampshire that had seen them occasionally walk past the picture window, the mother gasped and said, "That's exactly what the one up behind here was doing. He was swaying back and forth, peeking out from behind the tree I showed you."

Photographic or Eidetic Memory

We touched on this aspect earlier, but it deserves a bit fuller treatment. Imagine the level of precision with which Sasquatch must know its home turf in order to pull off constant mind-boggling feats of evasion and flawless terrain management. Many autistic savants, too, possess photographic memory, but none more prodigiously than Stephen Wiltshire, "the living camera," who was able to draw the city of Rome, in exquisite detail, after flying overhead in a helicopter just once. See "Beautiful Minds: Stephen Wiltshire."

In addition to Sasquatch's probable capacity to sense the presence of our technology through electroreception (as discussed in Part 4), it is likely as well that all of our "cleverest" attempts to conceal and camouflage game cameras are little more than sources of great amusement for them; if you have memorized every square inch of your territory, any change will stand out instantly, and dirty human tricks even more so—as though someone has just defecated in the middle of your living room rug.

Nor is being captured through photography and video their chief concern...

Mimicry or Echolalia

> Echolalia: the repetition of words, phrases, or sounds of the speech of others. Immediate echolalia is the exact repetition of someone else's speech, immediately or soon after the person hears it. Delayed echolalia may occur several minutes, hours, days, or even weeks after the original speech was heard. (AutismSpeaks.org)

This is another typical autistic impulse; Dawn Prince-Hughes recalls a childhood filled with "repeating conversations verbatim or singing my vast repertoire of commercial jingles. I loved the repetition and the symmetry of these commercials."

A strikingly similar phenomenon is experienced by people at Sasquatch habituation sites, as chronicled in *Our Life with Bigfoot*.

> North Carolina:
> They imitate my son, and say, "Mom!" loudly. They can sound just like him. I thought he was playing tricks, until they did it when I was here alone, and then when he was with me talking to me.

> Oklahoma:
> On many occasions, one of the kids will be outside and come running in asking, "Did you call me?" I have been working in the gardens or sitting outside and have heard a child's voice call, "Mom." It sounds just like

one of my kids. This has happened many times over the years when I was home alone.

Again, asserting and maintaining *control* is a cornerstone of autistic survival. It seems that in these episodes—as in all of their tricks and tactics—the hairy neighbors are also gaining control over situations in which they participate.

Iowa:
They mimic our voices too, all the time, to mess with us. The grandkids'll say, "We heard you hollering for us," and I'll say, "Oh…yeah." Again, I don't want to scare them.

Texas #1:
And they imitate my mom and say "Rachel" all the time. They will act like they are my dogs crying far away and as soon as I get far-far away looking for the dog they say "Rachel" back at the house, my mom's voice. Then when I get to the house my mom's not home, then they make the dog noise again, making me run back over and over till I give up. Just the other night, someone was mimicking my little brother calling for the dog. We hear that a lot.

Texas #2:
Then there was the voice trick. The girls would be at school and I would hear, "Mom!" from the woods. And I'd think, That couldn't be the girls because they're at school. But often, you know, it would be so real I would go and check just to see if maybe they got a ride home from school because they were sick? But we had to sign them out…

Or they'd be at home and come inside: "What do you want?" And I'd say, "What are you talking about?" So you know, these Forest People were imitating me and imitating them.

I think they'd just sit up in the trees and that was their entertainment. *Watch this one, watch that one.* Like a prank.

Also typical are instances of Sasquatch mimicking animal sounds, both (apparently) to "mess with" people and (certainly) to communicate with one another "under the radar." Many have reported hearing them "talk" back and forth in the chest-vibrating voice of "a three-hundred-pound owl." Researcher and linguist Scott Nelson visited a habituation site and heard "a nine-hundred-pound gobbler turkey. Another time, out there, I heard a nine-hundred-pound coyote. Scared the heck out of my son."

> Texas #2:
> I got on the second step of the porch and it sounded like I was transported to the Dallas Zoo, in the primate section. It started out with two "Woo Hoo Hoo Hoo!"—two of them doing that. And then it went to that screeching monkeys do when something's been taken away from them.
>
> I started looking around, and north of my house there were five large shapes moving in the trees. They were from about four-and-a-half foot up to I think eight, judging from the trees they were standing behind.
>
> There was a row of four-foot trees in front of them and much taller cedars behind them. That's when they started bird-whistling. And then they were frogs. I was getting these calls from just this one little section of the woods.

In this connection, recall "M.K. Davis discusses the crow caller video" and "M.K. Davis asks Does Sasquatch Mimic Human Speech?", and take a listen also to "Animal Mimicry near Sasquatch Structures" on YouTube channel Southern Ontario Sasquatch Research.

They possess an uncanny capacity to produce other sounds as well; a researcher friend of mine has heard a "motorcycle" start up in the middle of the night near his deep-woods campsite, where there are no roads.

> North Carolina:
> They imitated the sound of a babbling brook. Babbling brooks don't start and stop like you flick a light switch. And they also don't move. And during the course of the afternoon, as we looked around the place, the babbling brook followed us, which I just thought was funny.

Breaking Things

> Sasquatch like to break trees, bend them, push them down, and uproot them. The reason why they do this is unclear. (BFRO.net)

Photos by Sasquatch Investigations of the Rockies

Trees are sometimes found leaning roots-upward, leaning against other trees or even "replanted" upside down, like this one in CA

I think the behavior stems from the same source as their most carefully crafted structures. This may seem like a paradox, but it is not: In both activities, the underlying aim is to exert control over the environment. I well remember the habituator in East Texas telling me about nights filled with loud pandemonium near her house, trees being shattered with great force again and again, accompanied by excited vocalizations—"like they were having a party in there." The next morning, she'd check that part of the forest and, sure enough, find that "they'd trashed the place!" This phenomenon is reported wherever Sasquatch are regularly heard and glimpsed.

Depending on mood, one can assert oneself, stake a claim of authority, either by meticulously arranging one's world or else by becoming like a bull in a china shop. The latter raw display of power lets one master the moment, dominate the china shop—fighting chaos by *causing* chaos. In the autistic population, anxiety over lack of control can lead to similar mayhem.

- My son is walking around destroying everything he touches. He's not angry, just able. If left unattended he will rip apart a laptop, pour any liquid out anywhere, including on a TV. He threw the XBOX.

- My son is breaking all his pencils. He breaks them in half. I've asked him why and he says he needs to b/c it feels good.
- My son walks around the house literally tearing apart everything he can get his hands on. Our home is trashed 85% of the time because he is so destructive. (wrongplanet.net)

To hear three dramatic examples of explosive tree breakage in the ravine near me, check out the video "SLP Clip 5" on the GallowaySarah YouTube channel.

Organizing Space

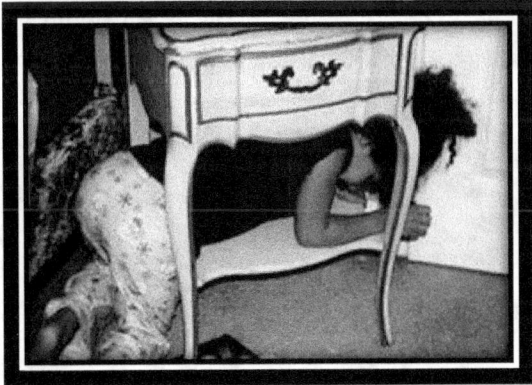

My friend Michael has explained to me how his clients tended to view space in the group home.

You and I look around at our house and think, "Okay, I'm in the house, this is my house, as a whole," but a lot of times an autistic individual will look at it as different sections in that house. They've broken it down. Their chair at the table. Their bedroom. Their bowl that goes on their shelf in their cupboard in the kitchen. They see it individualized into something personal. It gives them a sense of solidity.

If something of theirs is out of place, it's not "Oh, my stuff's out of place," it's a physical jolt. To avoid those feelings, they can compartmentalize. And then, if something new comes in, it changes everything. They have to re-associate themselves.

I think that space is of the utmost precious importance to Sasquatch as well; the sheer ubiquity and precision of their structures testify to this. All serious researchers are struck by how the forests are carefully carved up into separate sections and subsections. We have a thousand and one examples.

Perhaps the clearest have recently come from Colorado Bigfoot (Marc Abell). In addition to some of the finest structures ever filmed, he has shown barricades, blinds, fences, edging, and what he calls *perches*—spots where the soil has been obviously cleared and groomed in the midst of undeniable tree structures. See "Appreciating Colorado Bigfoot 2: Sasquatch Home Spaces" and "Appreciating Colorado Bigfoot 3: Sasquatch Groundwork."

Skeptics have pushed back, claiming that such rubbed-up locations are simply bedding sites for deer or elk. Abell's brief video "Sasquatch Seats in the Clouds" proves otherwise.

Even within the vast, remote territories accessed by Colorado Bigfoot, Sasquatch are evidently less expansive in their daily routines than they are conservative, repetitive, bounded—creatures of habit.

On wrongplanet.net, the chat topic "Small Spaces" includes these observations.

> For many years, I enjoyed getting inside small spaces. I have a small closet I like to get inside of. I've read that many people with autism like to get in small spaces or

wear pressure vests. It is quite comforting, but my question is why? What does this do for us that we like and how does it do this? Why is this comforting?

I think small spaces limit the amount of sensory input that I am exposed to. It's unlikely a little space will be messy or loud or bright. And that is usually what I am looking for, a dark, quiet cave to climb in to "escape."

Inflatable sensory pea pod

Most Sasquatch structures, as we have seen, are clearly insufficient as protection from the elements. Perhaps, instead, they function as occasional, embracing havens to hole up inside, affording not so much physical as psychological shelter.

17. *So What do Sasquatch Structures* Mean?

First, we need to look at the nature of meaning itself. For our purposes, there are two kinds: referential and non-referential. In referential meaning, the object in question points or refers to something else; examples would include a stop sign, a national flag, or the word *squirrel*. In non-referential meaning, the object in question carries significance in and of itself; examples would include a gem, the earth, or a Jackson Pollock painting.

In encountering Sasquatch structures, most researchers tend to emphasize the referential kind of meaning and try to puzzle out what a tree bend or wheel formation indicates—to crack some secret code. My own approach is quite different.

I think that Sasquatch woodcraft is produced for a variety of reasons that mutually complement and enhance one another. In addition to serving a referential function as trail and territorial markers, directional signs, family/clan "signatures," etc., or a pragmatic function as ambush hunting blinds, shelters, etc., I think they also (and primarily) fulfill an important emotional or psychological function. In many cases, there is no need to look beyond the salutary effect of the form itself; after all, for instance, everybody loves symmetry, but what does it mean besides…symmetry itself?

Marveling at the widespread and consistent formations documented throughout North America (and indeed, in many other regions of the world), what strikes me most is that this emphatic contouring of nature must answer a deep-set imperative. Everywhere they go, they are busily engaged in transforming their environment to suit their vision, apparently, of how it *should* look. This particular collection of archetypal designs and variations best proclaims and solidifies their identity; they naturally think *in terms of* such shapes.

Moreover, given their vulnerable position alongside *Homo sapiens*, their labors do make sense. If everywhere you look, you see your own handiwork winking back at you, the landscape becomes a warmly welcoming place, graced with expressions of self. You have personalized your world, making it more and more a home with each new creative flourish, even as the others, the outsiders, infect every horizon, threatening your safe and orderly sanctuary with danger and chaos.

You can catch glimpses into this form-based style of cognition by Googling and reading articles such as "Autistic People See Symmetry Better," "Autism Identified Early by Fixation on Geometry," and "Living in a Geometric Universe."

Painting by Patrick Jasper Lee, autistic artist

I think that the mind of Sasquatch follows a similar path. Our minds and theirs are flexible enough to use structures both referentially and non-referentially, just as we can respond both to a traffic signal and to a sculpture.

But when next you are stopped in your tracks by a hand-made manifestation in the forest, try not to limit yourself to asking, "What does it *mean*?" This will only obscure the genuine contact you are experiencing with the rich, abstract art of a kindred people—the beauty right before your eyes.

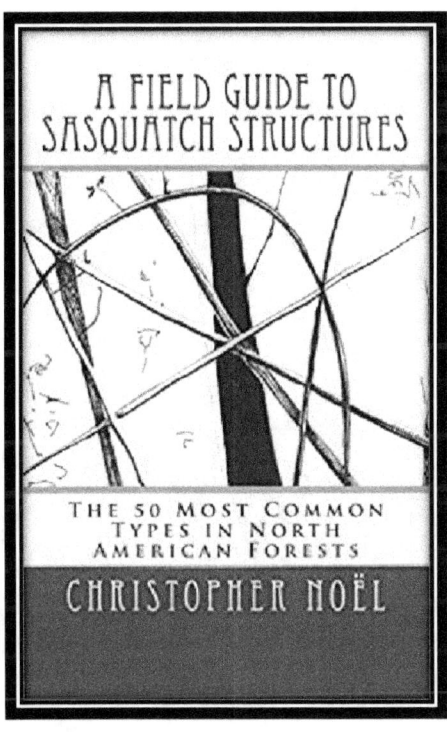

18. Autism as Naturally Selected?

Within evolutionary history, there may be a link between the Sasquatch's way of life—their hunter-gatherer prowess—and the earliest appearance and conservation of autistic traits in *Homo sapiens*. In *Rewiring Neuroscience*, Sam Harris suggests that autistics' "astonishing gift for visualization, memory, and pictorial thinking is an atavism—a re-expression or resurgence of an ancient style of thinking." In a fascinating 2011 article published in the journal *Evolutionary Psychology*, Dr. Jaren Edward Reser looks at autism from a fresh angle, not as a cognitive deficit but as instead conferring a survival advantage. If correct, this theory would mean that those occupying the autism spectrum today, though misfits in modern society, owe their "symptoms" to a proud pedigree. Reser proposes that

> some genes associated with the autism spectrum were naturally selected and represent the adaptive benefits of being cognitively suited for solitary foraging. People on the autism spectrum are conceptualized here as ecologically competent individuals that could have been adept at learning and implementing hunting and gathering skills in the ancestral environment.

> Young individuals on the autism spectrum may have been psychologically predisposed toward a different life-history strategy, common among mammals and even some primates, to hunt and gather primarily on their own. Many of the behavioral and cognitive tendencies that autistic individuals exhibit are viewed here as adaptations that would have complemented a solitary lifestyle.

> For example, the obsessive, repetitive and systemizing tendencies in autism, which can be mistakenly applied

toward activities such as block stacking today, may
have been focused by hunger and thirst toward
successful food procurement in the ancestral past. The
evolution of the neurological tendencies in solitary
species that predispose them toward being introverted
and reclusive may hold important clues for the
evolution of the autism spectrum and the natural
selection of autism genes.

PART 3

HOW TO "TALK" TO THE NEIGHBORS
CONNOISSEURS OF CONCRETE THINKING

19. Where Theory Meets Your Own Back Yard

The porch railing at SnowWhiteBigfoot's Ohio home (see section 21).

Despite the standoffish and relentlessly ghostlike nature of Sasquatch, it is quite possible to communicate with them.

When you enter into such a "conversational" project, however, it's important to avoid unrealistic expectations. Keeping in mind the behavioral and psychological qualities highlighted in Part 2 will help. To whatever extent you may or may not buy into my Sasquatch Savant Theory, the relationships forged at habituation sites do mirror those between an autistic person and a neurotypical person—but only up to a point.

Whereas in the case of human autism, breakthroughs occur that can open doors toward more straight-ahead access, this is not the case with Sasquatch; you will find no magic "gateway" as in the stuffed bear at Michael's group home. Even the most successful habituation relationships, which evolve and deepen over time, will never develop into anything resembling direct communion. Remember, the core concepts here are *indirection* and *mediation*. At its best, the rapport is intimate yet remote. From the human standpoint, the experience of outreach is like attempting to *get in touch with* a correspondent, and then, reaching this level, the most you can hope for is to *stay* in touch and to enjoy the texture and substance of the connection as far as it goes. Rather than focusing on the unbridgeable gap, pocket the gains as they occur. Your unseen counterpart is *interested* in you, for certain, and may even come to feel like family or a dear friend, displaying a distinct personality, a recognition of yours, and sharing with you repeated, familiar gestures and inside jokes.

When I write, in the title, "Next of Kin Next Door," the *door* in question does not swing open; we must operate through its keyhole. And when I write, in the subtitle, "How to Find Sasquatch," I mean *to find* in the sense of to find something *out* or to find *that* something is true. If Sasquatch could be simply located and met with in any unproblematic sense, the whole mystery would have vanished centuries ago.

20. How the Relationship Can Begin and Grow: Texas, Oklahoma, North Carolina, Montana

In the late 1990s, the East Texas habituation case began with odd changes and no way to know who was behind them.

> So there were a lot of things I would dismiss. Things being moved outside. I'd leave a hoe right there leaning against a tree near the garden. I'd go out there the next day to finish up and it's not there. And I'd find it out by the goat house hanging in a tree. And I'd think, Haven't y'all got something else to do besides mess with my tools? I was thinking about my daughters. I wish you girls would just leave shit alone. All the time. I would put all my flower pots in one area and I'd go back and half of them were gone or moved. Mostly I'd notice it overnight. (*Our Life with Bigfoot*)

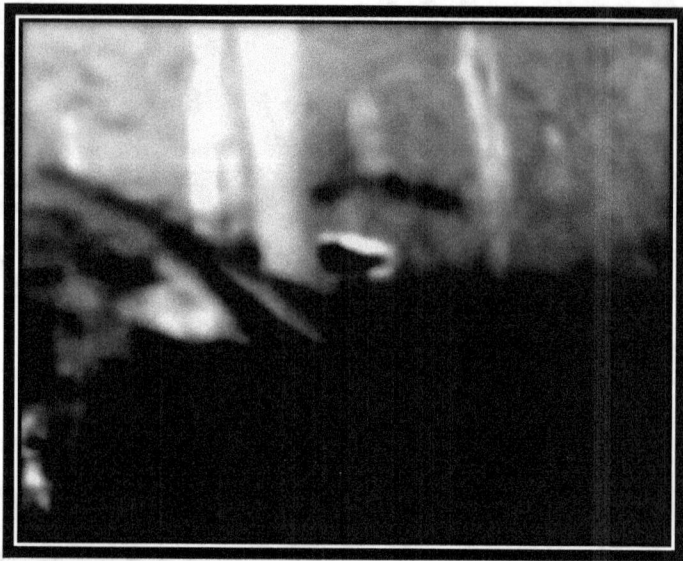

Years later, I obtained thermal footage at this property (see "Woodpile Sasquatch").

In "Sasquatch Fingerprints: East Texas Habituation Site (June 2011 Update)," I re-enact the original footage to contrast my head and arm with the subject's.

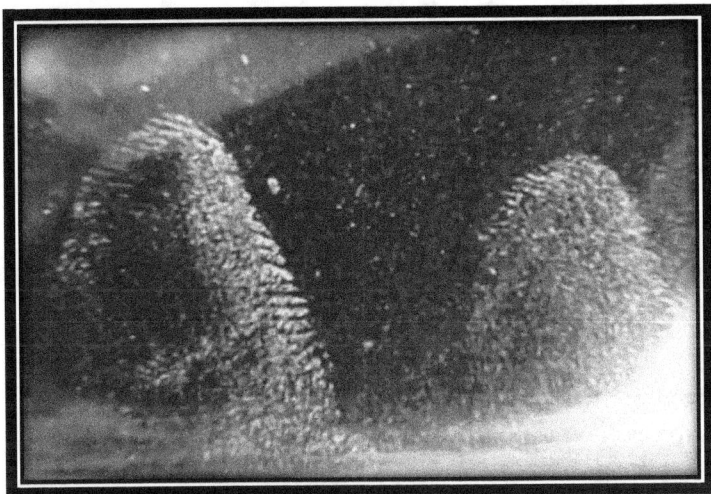

I also find non-*Homo sapiens* fingerprints on the back of my car.

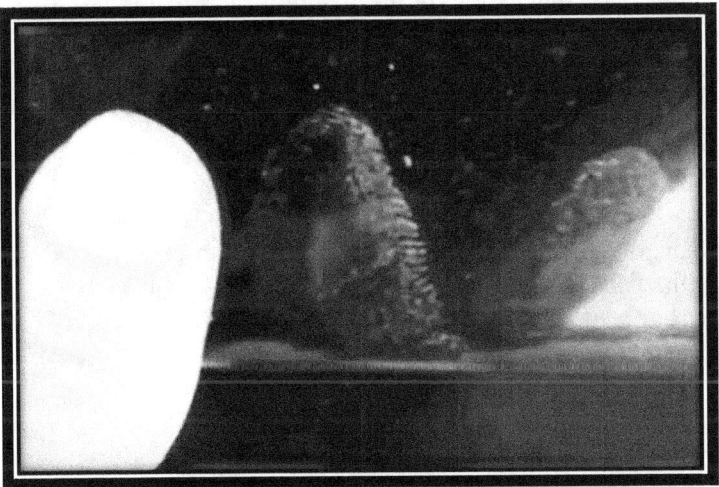

For a fascinating comparison to prints found at another site, see my video "Clear Sasquatch Fingerprints: Ohio and Texas."

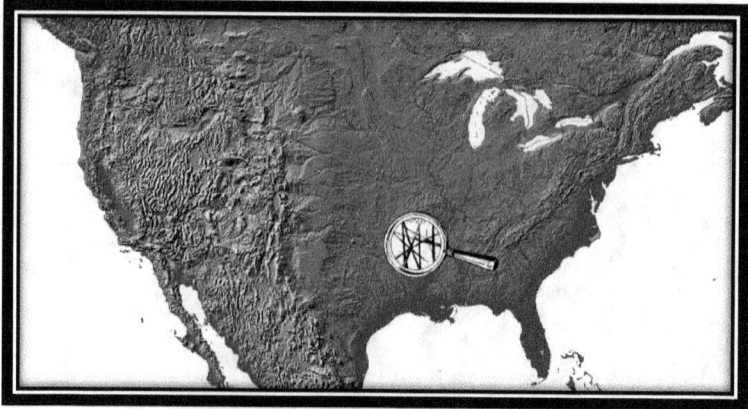

Also beginning in the 1990s, an Oklahoma family started noticing strange goings-on at their home.

I have always fed the wild animals. It's a hobby as much as compassion for the creatures the Creator has given us. This is a way of giving back to the Creator. We have so much and the little fur balls have so little. The more you feed, the more they will come.

Years back, we built a small garden pond, more of a frog sanctuary than anything. Stocked it with minnows and goldfish, which were promptly eaten. This was an ongoing pattern. Stock the pond and see how quickly the fish disappeared. A garden pond can be a great source of entertainment, also much work, depending on how you wish to handle it. Building an ecosystem takes time. As each spring came and went more was added to the pond. It was during this time that the prints began to appear around it. The first bare prints measured fourteen inches by five and a half inches. They appeared on the garden path beside the pond during the winter. They also appeared *in* the pond. As the footprints appeared the fish disappeared.

Each year the fruit would ripen. Just as it was ready to pick it would disappear overnight, never in the daytime. The bare footprints were different sizes. They ranged from a mere four inches long to nineteen inches long. The amazing thing about footprints: Often they are beside the paths, in the grass, as if to avoid detection.

In 2005, the resident shifted to a more documentary mode.

> Since the beginning of the year I have started to organize and keep a record of the Shadow People in my world. As the winter began turning to spring, I was recording audios and some videos, never catching a Shadow Person on film. Although I believe they did walk by chattering as in a conversation. This audio was shared with several others, including researchers, for evaluation. I have hope that someday there will be an answer to what sounded like a foreign language being spoken in my yard at two AM. I have had cameras moved, picked up, set down, and turned over.

> I began putting out snack food for the Shadow People. I tell them when I am putting it out that it is for them. They often are hiding in the woods nearby and I am certain they can hear me as I talk to them. At first, they didn't touch the snacks. This continued for several weeks.

> Then one night the snacks were taken. An audio recording of this indicated that during the rain the snack container was lifted out of the tree and returned. This container was approximately eight feet from the ground.

> Thus began the game of "snatch the snacks." Certain nights the snacks would be taken. Soon, I began attempting ways of catching the Folks on video. Never have I gotten more than a shadow moving or sounds that I have come to associate with the Shadow Family. On occasion I will have one container moved to another tree. Sometimes it will be higher or lower in the tree. Sometimes, I will need a ladder to take the container down to refill it.

> I also leave gifts of beads, toys, balls, and other interesting objects. Sometimes, toys and balls will

disappear for a period only to reappear months later. Sometimes the reappearance will last for only a day or two and then the objects will disappear again.

The toy house is a playhouse filled with abandoned toys not played with any longer. As the main house overflows with toys they are crated up and moved to the toy house. Only to be forgotten. This year I checked the toy house and found that most of the toys were no longer there. On occasion, I find small toys scattered over our acreage. Based on the behaviors I am observing, the Shadow People never take anything they know belongs to some member of the family. It appears they only take what is ignored. This not only includes toys. At times garden tools will disappear and reappear months later in an odd place.

There is no panic feeling. No fear. We continue about our business. I firmly believe that no harm will come to anyone who has a relationship with them. I will say never leave small children alone. Not because they will be harmed. Children can and will try to follow these guys.

Now, that being said, there are many reports of these creatures being frightening and dangerous. Yes that is probable and possible. I am always puzzled by these reports. What makes a creature, any creature, become aggressive? What makes a killer a killer? I will not dispute anyone's claim of aggression by a Bigfoot. I refuse to argue this point with anyone. I suspect that if there is aggression there is a reason for these actions. My thoughts are perhaps that aggression is due to getting too close to the young. Most animals, including humans, will protect their young by whatever means are at hand.

I have never witnessed aggressive behavior from the family unit that often visits us in the night. My family and I spend time out there at all hours of the day and night. Never while we are outside do we feel threatened. Watched, yes. I don't know how to describe it other than just that. Somewhere close by someone is watching.

It does, however, seem that the children and women more often have that feeling. There are possibly several reasons for this. One, the creatures watching are more interested in or entertained by children and women. Or possibly they withdraw further back when it's males about. I personally think that it's because men have a different air about them and are often the ones in the woods with guns.

I am not making a claim that the Shadow People live, reside or dwell on or near my property. What I do know is that they wander through at times. There have been several occasions in which we have gotten glimpses of them. Never the prized face-to-face.

There are times, especially at night, when I can tell the Shadow Folks are about. What can be said is if there is a whistle or click and it's verbally answered it will become quiet. Almost like an embarrassed quiet. The Shadow People have had millennia to perfect their camouflage. Like any creature, they adapt to the area they live in.

Until the last few years I had never tried to have a relationship with a giant creature. If you were to ask us to describe how we feel, knowing big hairy guys/gals are wandering the area, well you would get as many answers as there are people in the family.

The problem with a relationship with the gentle creatures of the forest, especially the larger ones, is a basic fear factor. It's built into each and every one of us. There is the fight or flight reaction. I would tell anyone who wants to know more: Take it slow and easy, there is no other way. This is a trust that slowly develops over time. We are talking about a creature that our Creator placed here with us. This creature to my way of thinking is on the same level as those of us without the constant hair shirt.

Habituation any way you want to present it is in fact a relationship. Started by one side or the other, for whatever reason. If you want a relationship with the Shadow People, remember they are intelligent.

I see no harm in gifting, but boundaries need to be established in habituation for the peace of mind and comfort of both sides. Never give what you do not want to be taken. Never set boundaries that you cannot live with. Remember, setting them may not even always work. They have had thousands of years to roam about. Just because you don't want one at your back door doesn't mean you have not somehow encouraged this behavior. Think before reacting. Overreaction will not help with any relationship.

I didn't start out to form a relationship with any animal in particular. I certainly never expected to have a tribe visit me in the middle of the night. I do feel that this is a very special gift from them to me that they have chosen our home as a respite at times.

Here's an example of a reaction that I can share. Recently in the middle of the night I was awakened several times to the sounds of scratching on the windows and sides of my home. Annoying, to say the least. This continued for several hours throughout the night. And what did the guys want? I have no idea. The scratching noise came to a halt with what sounded like a firm smack and a wounded baboon yelling and running away from the house. What I believe it to be was an errant child "pranking" and Mom becoming tired of this behavior and correcting it.

My reaction was getting up and actually taking the time to try to guess where it was coming from. Each time I turned on a light the noises stopped. As soon as the lights were turned off the noises began again. Did I see Bigfoot standing looking in the window? Nope! I do believe it was the family wandering about. I had left gifts of fruits and nuts for them.

As I started actually trying to communicate in some manner with the local Shadow People here, I tried many things. I have read many on-line conversations with many ideas on communicating with or "baiting" the big guys. A lot of these I dismiss as silly. The silly ideas generally are people who assume that these guys are of lower intelligence than us and must be treated on the level of a child, or a pet.

I fall back on treating the local Shadow People as I would want to be treated. I hate pushy know-it-alls. I avoid them myself. Using how I feel about neighbors and being a neighbor, I started with food and little gifts, which were often taken. I began to add other things: pebbles, feathers, ribbons, all of which have been moved around, relocated, or taken.

Then, one day, I wondered how roses would be received. I picked several rosebuds of different sizes and colors and included them with the other items. I found the buds the next day nearby where I had placed them. They had been taken apart petal by petal, and left.

A few days later, I awoke and went out to have coffee. I found a trail of pink rose petals to the area where my chair was. At the time I thought, Hmm, that is odd.

Later, I questioned my family about this. No one had done it.

On another morning, we found red roses lying on top of the car.

Several weeks after this, I again found a trail of rose petals from the front door to the patio. All in all, on three different occasions, I found a trail of pink rose petals scattered from the front door to the patio.

Often, the feeling of being watched is accompanied by soft sounds of movement. Sometimes sticks breaking or being pushed aside. It's at these times I try taking pictures of the area the noise is coming from. I have tried to school myself not to put a camera up to my eye or make a quick movement. Looking at photos taken at such times, I feel it is safe to say that most often what you will see in a photo is partial facial features. The eyes are what I notice most often. After finding an eye then I look for the other features.

One evening in the summer of 2007...
My nine-month-old grandson Squirt was sitting in the sandbox at the time of "the monkey-chase," as the kids called it. He was reaching and laughing at the bushes where they burst out. It was his behavior that got my attention at first. He was cooing and laughing as he reached out in that direction. I thought, Wow, he must see one of the cats.

A split second later, the first one burst out of the brush and ran bouncing across the yard. I am convinced Squirt had spent several minutes watching the monkey-kids in the edge of the brush. We call them that because they look like the drawings from the rise of man or the hobbits.

Just before dark, I saw three of them. The grandkids say there were five altogether, plus the babysitter. She was about the color of this little guy in the picture I took, maybe a bit more auburn.

I saw one very dark one, mouse-colored, and one red. The grandsons said there was actually three very dark ones and the two lighter ones. They were everywhere in a matter of seconds. It was one of the most amazing things I have ever had happen. They burst out of the bushes, ran all around us, and the kids gave chase like a game of tag. They won hands down. Then they were gone. They were between two and a half and three and a half feet tall, rail thin, and fast as the wind. Along with a female about five and a half feet tall hiding in the shadows and holding a baby. The babysitter kept reaching out from the brush as they would run by. She ran up and down in the brush. The most amazing thing is they never made a sound. None of them. As soon as it was over, my grandchildren put out a pizza and P&J sandwiches. Which disappeared right after dark.

Here's how I got a picture, on a different night. I usually just point the camera in the direction I hear noise, and if I can tell which way it's moving, I'll point it just ahead, where I think it's going to be. This night, we were sitting outside and then I heard some rustling and I started walking around the yard. It was well after dark. My daughter and I made a big circle around the yard just snapping pictures, and when we got over by the bench, we couldn't see him, we could just hear him moving around. I ended up with forty or fifty pictures and they were just dark. A friend of mine, another habituator, has a program where she can lighten them up, and she called me and said, "Guess what you got! You got a three-foot teddy bear walking around." I couldn't believe it. Then she asked me, "Does it look like he's holding something?" I'm thinking it's one of the teddy bears. They're about ten inches long. (*Our Life with Bigfoot*)

Juvenile Sasquatch photographed in nearly pitch dark, August 2007. The right hand holds a "borrowed" teddy bear; the left arm is in front of the body and thus not visible (don't be fooled by the bench frame). See the video "A Figure by the Bench: Oklahoma Habituation Site"

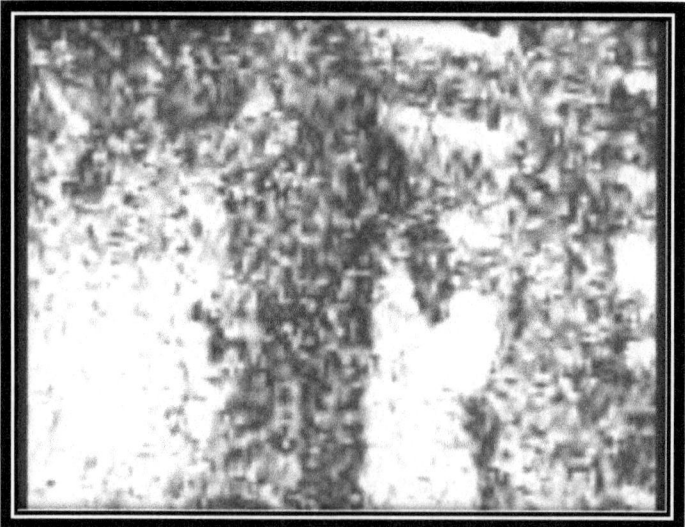

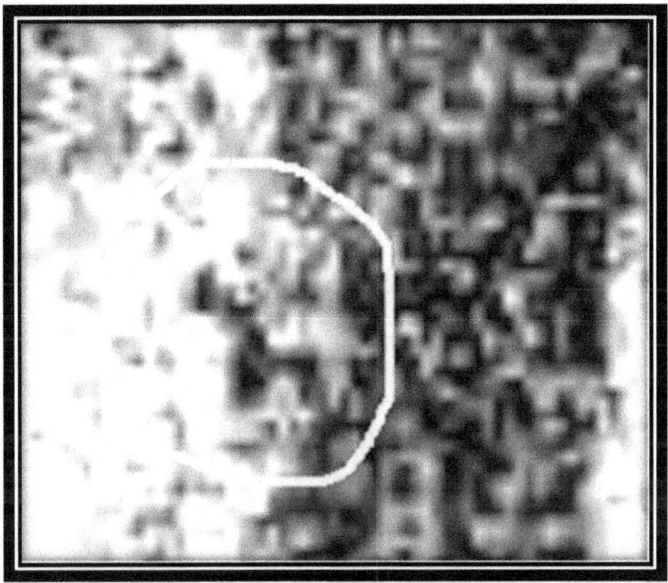

North Carolina is our next case study from the recent past.

It was back when we were living somewhere else, in 2002, and out here remodeling this house every day. Very first thing was a god-awful, gut-wrenching scream that came from our woods one day. My son and I both thought it sounded like a young child being raped or torn apart. There is an elementary school near here, and we believed someone was hurting a child in there. We both ran into that area of the woods, and looked, but saw nothing. I went back to the field, to make sure someone wasn't getting away, and my son continued to look around in that area of the woods. He said he never saw anyone, but it looked like someone had been there, because a lot of plants and grasses were laid down and flattened.

We heard the same scream, in the same area, a few days later, but same results, on searching. There was an obvious path we hadn't noticed before, so my son checked the area off and on, at random times for about a week.

Then, from different parts of the woods over different times, we'd hear what we thought was humans trying to break into the place or coming up here. We weren't staying over here all the time, like I said. We thought there were people running through the woods. We shot at them. We've called the Sheriff's Department out here several times, too many times. Nobody ever found anything. My son chased them, never could catch up with anybody. And that went on for a long time.

What really brought it to a head was, we rented a backhoe and went to dig the ditches, and when I did that they started throwing stuff at me. Mud and sticks. I really didn't know what was going on, so I had some BFRO investigators come out. They came out three different times and did an overnight. The first time they came out they found footprints and they did some hollers and got some answers, did some wood-knocking and got some answers, and that kind of blew us all away.

We were like, Oh okay, we got Bigfoots. I mean, we kind of thought the place was haunted for years. But then once we found out, my son and I just really got interested in it. We started trying to study them. Daily. We started going out there and trying to communicate with them, and basically just went from there.

I've got one group on one side of the house that's

pretty receptive and friendly and we've come quite a ways. On the other side, behind the barn, they're mean. I've only been doing this about three months.

I've been watching my woods change here daily. In all these years I've only ever seen them three times. You would just have to experience the thickness of my brush. You could hide an elephant in there.

I believe what makes them stay here is that our area is very quiet, with a good source of food and water. There's not a lot of traffic. We don't go out in the woods a lot. They've been here before we were here. It's not that they moved in, they just didn't move out.

The nice ones, when I feed them, sweet potatoes and apples and bananas, they sometimes leave me gifts. I keep them all in a small bowl. Pretty rocks. One of the rocks is studded all through with large garnets. One looks like some kind of petrified bone...maybe a hip and part of the socket, from some little animal. The rest are lots of quartz, and some is just plain rocks. I also got a civil war grapeshot cannon ball, and half of some kind of old metal bullet mold. And I got a little ceramic duck that looks like it has spent some time in the swamp.

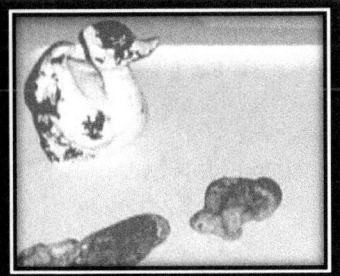

The mean ones, out behind the barn, they killed my dog and left me his skull and some bones on the work table over there. He must have been bothering them.

It was very hard to accept, but we moved on. I have had worse times. You get over stuff, and move on.

I want to let people know that there are some down sides to this too. I will study them while they stay, but if they moved on tomorrow, I would just get back to a "normal" life here. I wouldn't go looking for them anywhere else. Some days I don't want to deal with them here. But I try to keep it steady, so I can learn more.

It's a whole game of building trust with them, and it doesn't just include handing them food and walking away. People would probably think I was crazy. I go out there and I talk to the woods. I walk around, I speak to them, I sing to them, my son plays guitar for them. He's twenty-two. He and I are the only ones doing the study here.

I definitely know they know when I'm there. I think they know every time I step out this door because I hear them whistle. They give little whistles to I guess kind of let each other know that you're coming out.

From area to area in the yard they whistle the same way. Different little whistles different places. (*Our Life with Bigfoot*)

See my video "Faces in the Foliage: North Carolina Haibtuation Site."

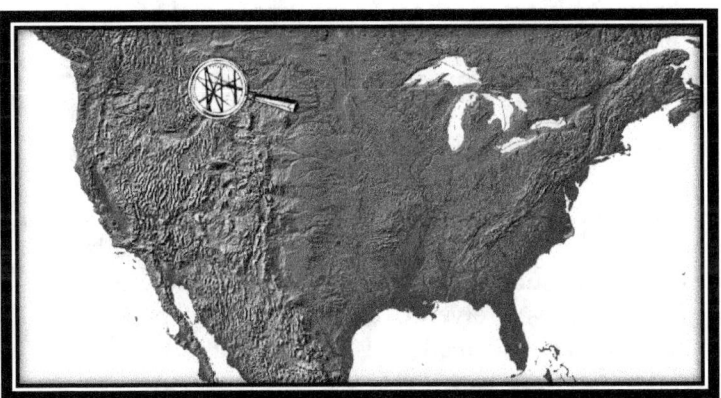

This Montana experience was recently chronicled in an episode of "Bigfoot Eyewitness Radio: Non-Stop Sasquatch Activity." The speaker is a woman named Robin, whose encounters began in 2011, when she was thirty-nine years old.

> I'm glad that it happened when I was older so that I could wrap my head around it a little better than if I were a younger person.
>
> When my daughter was two, she started talking about these "dog friends" that would come to the window and tap and wanted her to open the doors, and we would have just this constant noise. This was when I said to my aunt, "There's something going on and I want you to hear this." So she came over and it was just this constant banging. It was coming from the roof, from the sides of the house…we were surrounded by banging. We had substantial roof damage. It looked like something had just crumpled parts of the roof like aluminum foil, and you could hear bolts popping off. It

was so unsettling. At the same time, I was finding very large footprints all over the property and handprints on the doors. And it's not like a normal handprint. It was very greasy and oily, and I had to use straight vinegar to get it off.

We had this flavored lip gloss for little kids. It smells really good, like grape or Doctor Pepper, and I kept all those in my truck when my daughter was little because she liked to put them on her lips. I'd come in my truck and they'd all be eaten. They would somehow get into my truck, get those lips glosses, and just start scarping them out, and there was nothing left. It's in a tube, so even down to the bottom…it must have been a little one, because the fingers have to be pretty small, unless they used a stick or something. I'd find all these empty lip balm tubes. We've woken up with car doors open and trunks open and all kinds of crazy stuff.

The things that the Sasquatch do are based on curiosity. They like to play pranks on us. They'll hide things. They like to observe people. They know us better than we know ourselves in a sense. They know our habits. For instance, they know that I like rocks. I have a rock collection that I have outside, and they will move rocks around. I'll go outside and one of my favorite rocks (about ten pounds) will be on the other side of the house. Things like that that are subtle, they're not subtle to me because it's what I like

They do things like that with my daughter, too, where if she leaves a toy outside, it's gone. And then days later, sometimes a month later, it will come back, and it will be in a flower pot. They've been missing for months and then suddenly they're back. Or she'll suddenly have this new toy. "Well, where did you find that?" "Oh, it was in the garden." They'll bring her things that they find. Who knows where they find stuff? But they'll bring us these crazy little gifts. It's never a dull moment. You have to be really on your toes with them around.

When I'm outside, I'm usually pretty aware. We have bears and mountain lions and things. I was outside and I saw in the tree line, kind of back a little bit, this very large figure, and it was white. White in the forest really stands out. We have a branch that measures about eight feet tall, and this figure was dwarfing that branch. And very muscular, very *very* muscular. At the time, I was still very scared. When this starts happening to you, no matter how prepared you think you are, you're not prepared to see something that big, that massive, in front of you. This was maybe five yards away, where you can see hair blowing in the breeze, you can see the face, you can see eyes. You can see muscles underneath the hair, and it's very clearly built like a person. The only difference is that it did not have a neck. But even as recessed as it was in the trees, you could see the eyes, and their eyes are intelligent. It's not like looking into the eyes of a doe or the eyes of a horse or the eyes of anything we would consider to be an animal. Even dogs. We love our dogs, but there's a big difference. This was *someone*. And he just walked away.

My daughter says, "Mommy, they blend in with the trees, and that's why you can't see these friends. Sometimes the little ones go up *in* the trees, but the big Mommy and the big Daddy just blend into the trees. Or they get down on their bellies."

And she said, "And you can't see them unless they want you to." With the texture of their hair, I can see how they would be able to blend in with bark and with grass and with forest litter.

I never take it for granted that this is a very special relationship, and I do whatever I can to preserve it because there's a very high level of trust that goes both ways. And there's also a protectiveness that I feel towards them.

It's not until I travel and stay in a hotel that I realize how abnormal life is at my home, because there are nightly taps on the windows or slaps on the side of the house. And it makes me a little melancholy, not to have those knocks.

And normally when it's a loud slap, I know that they'd like my dog to come out and play, and I'll let him out, and he'll be gone for an hour, and then he'll come back so tired and he'll have a treat with him. They'll give him bones. Sometimes, if it's summer, he'll have oil on him too. Their hands, I think, get really oily, and you can see where he had an oily hand print, and then dust settles on that hand print.

My daughter seems to see them the most. She'll be out, jumping on the trampoline, and she'll just say, "Oh, there they are. They're in the trees," or "They're in the woods, watching." It's not a serious issue, but she'll have her friends come over and she'll see the Sasquatch in the tree line, watching her and her friends. I think it's just a matter of time before her little friends are seeing them too. So it makes for a very interesting life out here.

In my mind, it's just like having family there, and I've spoken with other people that have Sasquatch on their property where they have this kind of a relationship, and they say the same thing, that it's almost like it's an extension of your family. A friend of mine will leave them little gifts of things that they like, and then when they're out of whatever it is, they'll bring back the empty container, like they want more, more of that item. So it's comforting to know that I've found other families that have this going on, too, and that my family experiences this as well, because if I were here by myself, I'm pretty sure I'd think I was a little off my rocker.

I was about to install outside lights and game cameras, but I'm glad I didn't. I would have completely undermined my relationship with them. It makes you focus on getting them away from you and from your house. But they haven't done anything that would endanger my family, and I don't want to live in a prison. This is one of my most treasured relationships because it is so unique and it makes me have faith in a lot of things. If they're possible in the world, think of what else might be out there, and I don't want to jeopardize it at all.

When you have knowledge about something, that arms you. Knowledge is power, and I feel very much empowered now.

I never knew they built things until after we cleared the field beside our yard, cut down the tall grass and geranium bushes. There's a river running the length of our property, and a trail goes down the embankment and then along the river. We stopped our clearing right at that trailhead, and then the next day, we went down to the river. Where there was nothing before, now there was this huge tree pushed down and blocking that trail, and there were all these smaller trees and branches interwoven into that. This was a healthy tree, and there's no way it would have just suddenly flopped over. And with all the smaller trees and branches and saplings from other parts of the property all woven in, this structure was impassable. We called it "the roadblock." My dad looked at it and said, "Well, I guess this side is ours and that side is theirs." It very clearly was a boundary, like they recognized what we'd been doing up top, that they weren't allowed to come near the house, and they did the same thing down here. To us, this felt like a communication of understanding.

We also had trees turned upside down, with the roots in the air, across the creek from us. And we've had branches that were as thick as a man's arm snapped, twisted, and woven around something else, but at eight or nine feet off the ground. And there are stick structures all over the place.

Robin's brother Aaron contributes his perspective as well.

There's this one Sasquatch that, when it's around me, conveys that to me with this intense feeling. It starts in my chest and just grows from there to go throughout my entire body. It's so intense and so…I guess you'd say *full*. And I'm not fearful. At times, when I hear knocking on the house, I'll go outside and see what's going on. At this point in our situation, I'm kind of inviting more interaction, wanting to have more of a type of communication and to be more open. They mean no harm, and they're probably just as curious as we are. I'd like to know more about them. I'm the type…I seek solutions, I problem-solve. I would like this to be more open, but they have their own way.

Yes, they certainly do have their own way, and this is why communicating with them requires a very specific set of "social" skills vastly different from those we employ in ordinary life. In the four examples above, the common theme is the manipulation of objects. In Texas, the resident found the relocation of garden tools baffling and annoying; in Oklahoma, toys were the currency of exchange, but far more personally, the woman of the house experienced touching overtures in the form of rose petals; in North Carolina, the dynamic was both positive and very negative, including numerous gifts but also a malignant act (the dog used as a meaningful "object"); and finally, in Montana, the little girl routinely had her toys "borrowed" then returned, and she would receive things she'd never seen before: "Who knows where they find stuff? But they'll bring us these crazy little gifts."

Willingly or not, countless people have been experiencing these object-based interactions throughout North America for who knows how long, but nobody has chronicled such an experiment in communication with more consistent focus, record-keeping dedication, and attention to detail than the researcher who posts as SnowWhiteBigfoot.

21. A Loving Lab in Ohio

SNOW WHITE BIGFOOT

To paraphrase Emily Dickinson, "Minds in the same ground meet by tunneling." This is what it's like to successfully conduct an ongoing exchange of messages and meaning with a Sasquatch or small group thereof. It is a long process with numerous fruitless passages. Keep on digging. As you will see below, this woman in Ohio is tireless in her efforts to draw nearer and ever nearer to her unseen visitors. Fortunately, there are rules to follow when you feel lost.

1. Great patience is required. These exchanges do not unfold in a compressed time frame like a chess match; though you are quick to respond to any change, it may be days or weeks before the next "move" on the other side of the "board." The metabolism of this cryptic alliance becomes a way of life.

2. The process often—though not always—proceeds is an extremely subtle key. Strict attention to detail can reveal shifts that are at once minor, precise, and intelligent, even humorous. Taking note of nuances will allow you to keep up…and to respond in kind.

3. The game will be end abruptly if you make sneaky false moves, such as tucking a GPS tracker into a gift or installing surveillance cameras. (They don't seem to mind audio recorders, however; see Part 5.)

4. Do not offer them "treats" that are not part of their natural diet, such as junk food and refined sugar.

5. Attitude is everything: humility, appreciation, and open receptivity are a must. An egocentric stance or ulterior motives will seriously curtail the interaction, prevent it altogether, or even perhaps turn your visitors nasty. (I'm not suggesting that the North Carolina resident herself brought on the killing of her dog; like people, Sasquatch can be unpredictable, with varying personalities and their own reasons.)

6. Understand, finally, that the entire venture is *on their terms*. They are the prime movers here, in charge of time table, rhythm, and tone. Forgetting this will distort your sense of what's going on, often making you feel slighted

or rejected, which in turn may sour the atmosphere for all concerned. It's not about you, don't mope.

SnowWhiteBigfoot follows these rules to a T. Her years-long habituation process is chronicled as "My Bigfoot Diary" and comprises thirty-six installments thus far. Since its total running time exceeds twenty-five hours, I'm aware that some may find it a challenge, so I'll lend a hand.

For an overview, check out "How to 'Talk' to the Neighbors" on my YouTube channel (Impossible Visits).

Until you get hooked on SWB's diary entries, I'd recommend starting with Part 7: "Gifting: Let the Bigfoot Games Begin." As of Part 9, she includes a companionable voice-over that makes the viewing experience more immersive.

Here are some highlights not to be missed. These are just a handful out of many I could have chosen, but I trust they will inspire you to take in the entire series.

- Part 10—5:44-6:55; 14:42-15:35
- Part 11—23:28-24:32
- Part 12—12:46-14:12; 17:20-18:51
- Part 13—12:04-13:41
- Part 14—11:25-12:00; 23:56-25:57
- Part 15—7:37-8:56
- Part 16—2:14-2:29; 3:03-5:25
- Part 17—5:08-6:32
- Part 18—14:58-17:21; 19:15-20:26
- Part 19—4:27-4:59; 11:28-11:59
- Part 20—10:00-10:48
- Part 21—13:11-4:14; 16:18-17:07
- Part 22—2:28-3:08
- Part 23—10:51-12:00; 18:53-21:00
- Part 24—58:14-58:57
- Part 25—00:00-4:56; 14:40-15:36; 20:00-21:24
- Part 26—15:37-16:51; 44:39-46:00

- Part 27—00:31-1:22; 26:11-33:23; 40:36-43:23
- Part 28—19:47-20:40
- Part 30—20-41-25:40; 30:51-33:1; 34:59-35:42
- Part 31—33:52-35:10; 38:06-end
- Part 32—23:36-28:30; 35:21-36:52
- Part 33—12:21-14:00; 19:26-22:39

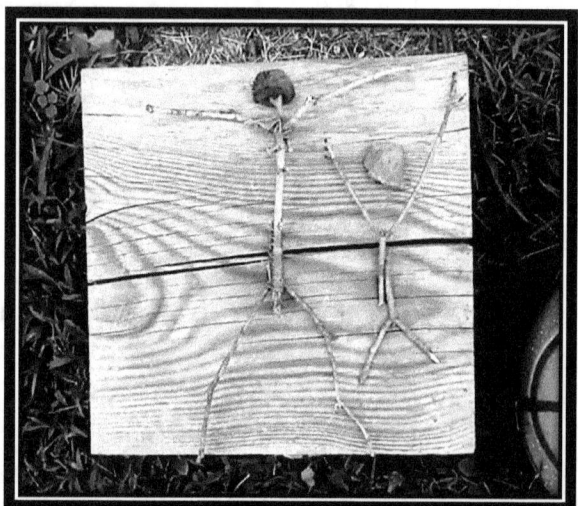

SWB left a stick man and then found a companion figure added (on the right).

Frequently, her husband Jim's tools are returned after being "borrowed" or tools will appear that he's never seen before.

Sometimes, they will add gifts that match objects SWB has left out.
SWB had never seen the near ball before.

She has conducted with them a long-running
game of "change the dice"...

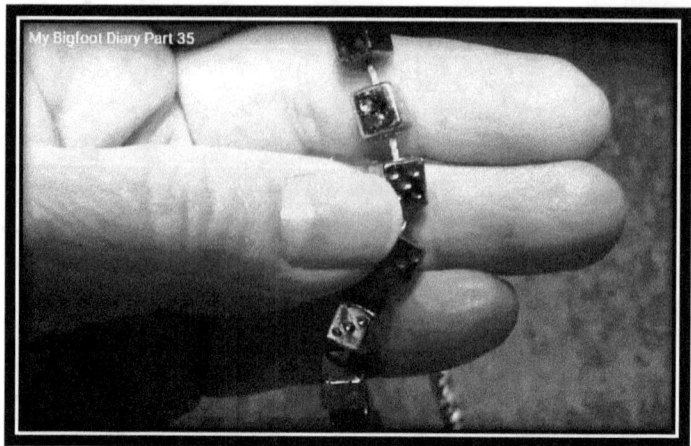

...and, astonishingly, they have gifted her this necklace.

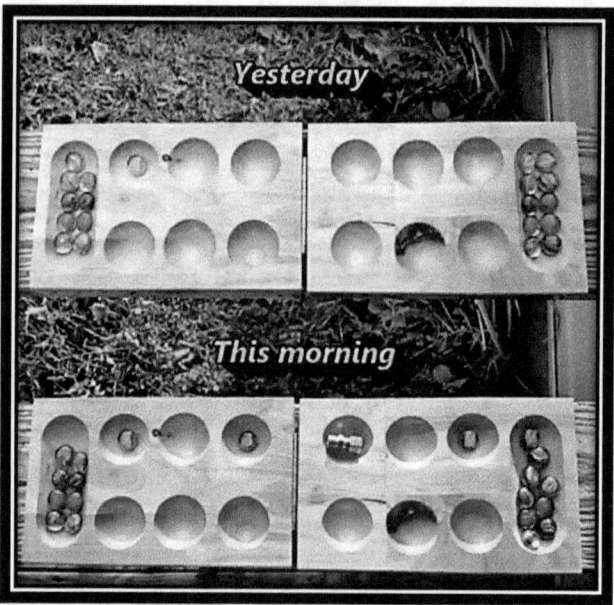

Using a mancala game, SWB prompted her visitor to take a turn; he or she added two blue marbles and a brass fitting.

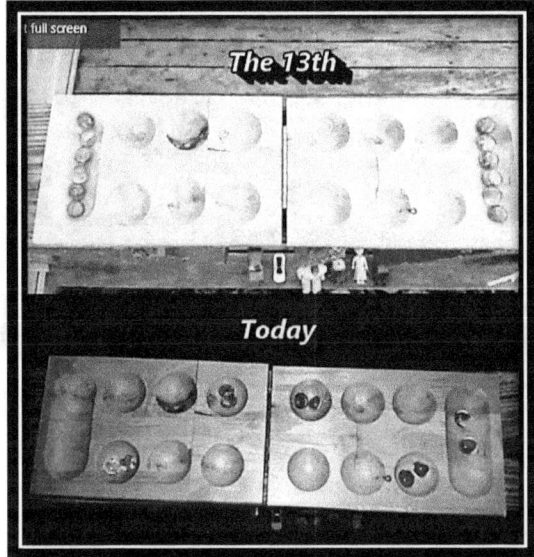

Sometimes, the changes are more elaborate.

SWB left out an unopened jar of peanut butter...

...and found it with its lid removed, its seal peeled back, and a stick shoved in.

She left out a tub of sand to see what would happen...

...and soon found a tiny footprint; someone had been standing with one foot in the sandbox and one foot out on the grass.

She was able to cast the print; the toes are clearly visible.

As you will see, in between such rousing moments of surprise and delight are lengthy stretches filled only with modest, repetitive routines, reliable patterns; among numerous examples, small gifts are forever being left at the center of SWB's porch chair, and the magnetic silver bowl is placed upside down beneath the hood of the grill with astonishing regularity.

One can't help thinking of OCD—a syndrome often associated with autism—and yes, it is actually possible to find yourself feeling unimpressed by the sameness of these moves if, for a moment, you allow yourself to forget that they represent the very *ideas and gestures of Sasquatch.*

But this feeling itself is strangely instructive. The mere fact that this thingly dialogue can become even remotely tedious at all testifies, again, to the nature of the "beast." They are certainly capable of being aggressive and terrifying—that occasional bull in the china shop—but on the whole, they are far more monotonous than monstrous. And I mean this word in the sense of producing a *monotone*, one note, a single underlying behavioral theme (with variations).

This theme is control.

In fact, some of the *least* monstrous attributes of our own species—patience, situational awareness, subtlety, careful judgment, precise attention to detail—are what Sasquatch possess in greater abundance than the average human being; otherwise, they'd never have been able to accomplish what they have over the centuries and on a minute-to-minute basis. Autistic people, too, of course, exude these qualities, engaging in exact, recursive routines to orchestrate their days and shape their world.

Another aspect of SWB's ongoing project sheds light on *their* side of the equation, too. Because new items, never before seen, are continually appearing on the porch railing, we can infer that the Sasquatch are obtaining them elsewhere, and since these are often tools, little toys, marbles, and fun pieces of jewelry, it's safe to assume that they came from other households. Add to this the fact that SWB's and Jim's own belongings frequently disappear, either temporarily or permanently, and we can make the following educated guess: Area habituation sites participate, without quite realizing it, in a system of rotating objects; in Part 32 of "My Bigfoot Diary," inside the grill (beside the metal bowl), SWB finds a wrench that had been left at Jim's parents' house more than a month earlier and four miles away.

Each Sasquatch group that puts itself on the field of play like this is likely conducting numerous similar games locally with those neighbors who have shown a similar inclination—those at each address probably assuming that they alone are thus blessed with invisible playmates. It's like a chess grandmaster who is able to match wits with dozens of opponents simultaneously. In this manner, your periodic partner(s) can stay engaged and mentally stimulated while making the rounds, yet remain a constantly moving target, distributing and diminishing the risk.

Many habituators attempt to read specific messages in the configurations they find on their property, and in some cases a plausible interpretation is possible; SWB ventures many herself. Most of the time, however, I think it's best to accept each fresh manifestation as a good-humored gift that means essentially, "I acknowledge you."

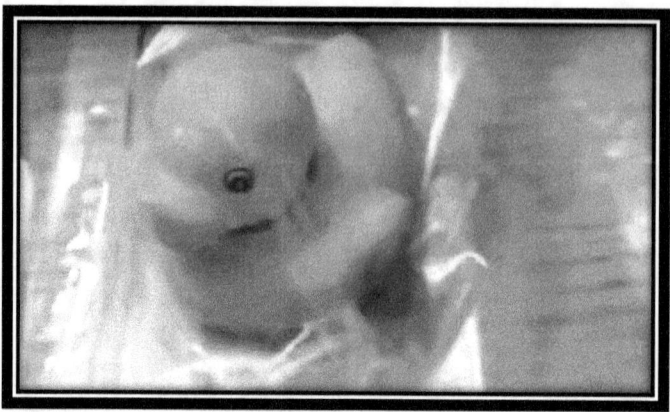

SWB keeps all the gifts carefully preserved and labeled; see her video "My Bigfoot Treasures, Who is Habituating Whom?"

Through the years, here on this researcher's porch, we see the role of concrete thinking, a focus on objects as the primary currency of exchange. Her local visitors do seem aware of her— what she appreciates and what she offers—but there's also little doubt that their sights are set at the level of the game itself.

A quick check of some secondary sources shows that the human autistic mind, too, leans heavily in this direction. Leo Kanner, the psychiatrist who coined the term *autism* in 1943, wrote that

> Objects that retain their sameness and never threaten to interfere with the child's aloneness are readily accepted by the autistic child. He has a good relation to objects. The children's relation to people is altogether different. Every one of the children [in my study], upon entering the office, immediately went after blocks, toys, or other objects, without paying the least attention to the persons present. It would be wrong to say that they were not aware of the presence of persons. But the people, so long as they left the child alone, figured in about the same manner as did the desk, the bookshelf, or the filing cabinet. (Kanner, 1985)

Further strong resemblance to SWB's experience emerges from an article called "Developing Play in Children with Autism."

Play in children with autism looks different from play in neurotypical children. Their play seems to be repetitive and unchanging. For example, they may play with the same toy in the same way over and over again. They may line things up or move objects in and out of containers. Much time is spent on simple manipulative play. (autismwestmidlands.org.uk)

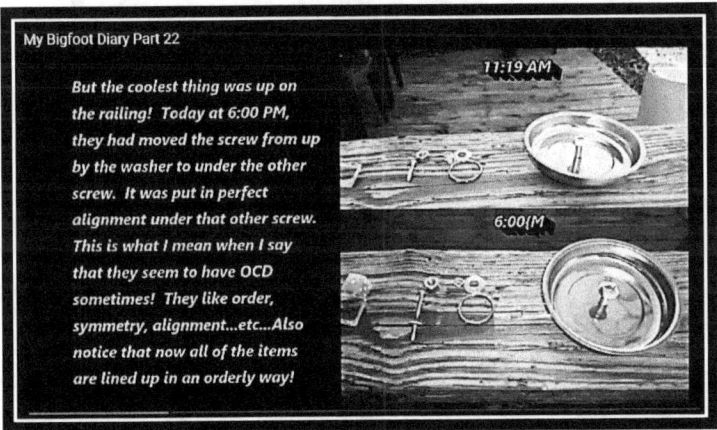

My Bigfoot Diary Part 22

But the coolest thing was up on the railing! Today at 6:00 PM, they had moved the screw from up by the washer to under the other screw. It was put in perfect alignment under that other screw. This is what I mean when I say that they seem to have OCD sometimes! They like order, symmetry, alignment...etc...Also notice that now all of the items are lined up in an orderly way!

11:19 AM

6:00{M

"They had moved the screw from up by the washer to under the other screw...in perfect alignment. This is what I mean when I say they seem to have OCD.... They like order.... Notice how all the other items are lined up in an orderly way!"

The Indiana Resource Center for Autism almost seems to be channeling SWB's methods when it recommends that

> If a child is fixated on lining up blocks, the adult should join in and add blocks to the child's line. Then the adult may place a block perpendicular and start the line going in a different direction. When the child continues the new line, he/she has "closed the circle of communication." If a child has very limited play themes, it may be helpful to use sensory toys (e.g., sand tables).

And finally, another online community echoes many habituators' mild frustration with the ongoing sameness of their communicative results. As you will have noted in "My Bigfoot Diary," the selfsame gestures are replicated time and time again.

> Once engaged, a child with autism will often prefer to do the same things over and over again, and it can be hard to break the pattern. (verywell.com)

Autistic boys often show an attachment to model cars.

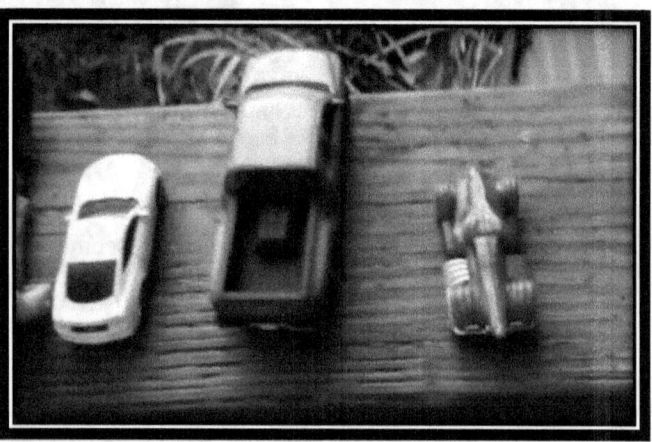

In Part 30 of "My Bigfoot Diary," from the 35:00 mark, a new car has been added to the row (far right), never before seen here.

Through all of this rich yet circular interaction, however, SWB's mischievous company has never once allowed her or her husband to *see* them, though her stepson and his girlfriend did score a lucky break one night: "Bigfoot Sighting at the End of Our Driveway; August 3, 2017."

At my own place here in Vermont, I caught a glimpse once, but only the most fleeting one imaginable.

22. Retaliation behind my Tool Shed: Examples of What Not to Do

T-pee structure in the woods beside my yard

As you may have seen in the video "How to 'Talk' to the Neighbors," I myself have been graced by occasional remarkable overtures here at my home, twelve miles from Montpelier. Though these have not come at remotely the pace as at the Ohio site—nor do I possess SWB's work ethic!—I have appreciated each one.

But this past summer, I think I ruined the trust relationship through ego and thoughtlessness. I simply did not follow the rules.

My first mistake was to place a "spy" camera aimed at the t-pee. The next day, a tree came down on the structure, breaking one of its beams.

Five weeks later, my second mistake was apparently even worse. I left half of a cranberry walnut coffee cake beside the path where I'd recorded bipedal steps and breathing; see "Just How Heavy Are Sasquatch Footsteps?"

Two mornings later, my offering was gone.

And then, that very night, at 10:07, aided by no wind at all, a huge tree crashed to the ground. I heard it from inside my house. And can you guess where that tree had landed? That's right, the t-pee structure was destroyed; see "Sudden Changes behind the Tool Shed 7: Throwing the Hammer Down."

What's the moral of the story? Don't try to trick them into appearing on video, and don't give them food, such as pure sugar, that is likely to make them sick…and furious.

Pre-coffee cake, however, I did once catch sight of my visitor. Well, I didn't see him in real time, but later, the footage revealed a split-second mistake while he was spying on *me*. (Double standard? Yes!) For just a few frames, his shaggy arm is visible between two trees, and then it's quickly withdrawn. "Sudden Changes behind the Tool Shed 4: A Glimpse" shows that the word "quickly" is an understatement—and that "exposure anxiety" is on full display here.

23. A Long Tradition

Stories of attacks were probably exaggerations born of fear.

Few modern-day habituators realize that they represent just the tip of an historic iceberg. Gift exchanges with Sasquatch— known by a wide variety of names, including *werewolf, forest spirit, nature god, shape-shifter, troll, green man*—are certainly nothing new, both here in North America and throughout much of the world. How can we know this? Because those habituation projects I have followed, and there have been dozens, all started out quite naturally. It seems to be a basic human duality, when in the presence of a wild, uncanny version of oneself, either to recoil or to reach toward contact, and among the latter group, we find ourselves compelled to understand, to seek a common language that may allow for familiarity and reciprocation—to form a *relationship*.

Unfortunately, no early rendition of "My Bigfoot Diary" has

surfaced from the Middle Ages, but in brief historical references we can find little keyholes into a rich backstory.

> Werewolf legends appear to have originated in the German countryside around Cologne and Bedburg in the year 1591. Many claimed to have found torn limbs on their properties and scores feared to travel in the surrounding wooded areas. (Maryann Paige, "Werewolves and the Middle Ages," ezinearticles.com)

> The bogeyman finds its genesis in the old central European gods. After Christianity came to central Europe and made its way to the British Isles, many of the deities from previous beliefs became evil spirits. It is natural to assume that the gods of pre-Christian Britain became known as these nasty, horrible, frightening or mischievous beings—ancient pagan gods, demons and devils, bogs, bogeys, or boggles. There was a time when a saucer of milk or a slice of bread left outside the door at night became an offering to the old gods. (The BBC Homepage)

In the next example, which occurred between 1835 and 1850, the residents were not interested in playing along, but the situation apparently would have been ripe for such participation.

> It all began shortly after Sam Houston and his army had secured independence from Mexico for Texas. Settlers who had fled from the advancing Mexican army now returned to their homesteads and were starting over. It was about this time that odd tracks began turning up near various settlements and homes along the Navidad River. There were usually two sets of tracks, one pair larger than the other and always barefoot, so it was widely assumed the prints belonged to a male and a female. Sometimes they appeared in the sweet potato or cornfields where the pair helped themselves to some of the bounty secured by the labors of the sod-busting settlers. No one ever saw this pair. It seemed they took great pains to avoid detection.

A couple of years passed and the barefoot tracks of
the larger individual ceased to be seen, but the tracks of
the smaller individual continued to appear in the potato
fields of the area. In fact, the visits seemed to increase
in frequency. The people of the community wondered
if this might not be due to the fact that the "woman"
was not as adept at finding game as her mate had been.
For various reasons, ranging from a desire to help this
recluse to mere curiosity, a plan was hatched by
several of the young men in the area to lie in wait and
capture the wild woman. One night, as they hunkered
down in a potato field, she came. The night was dark
but the men claimed they could discern the figure of a
woman, apparently unclothed, cautiously approaching
their location. When she had drawn near to them they
sprang in an effort to capture her with their bare hands.
They drew nothing but air, however, as the woman,
exhibiting impressive agility, dodged, ducked, and
quickly bounded away without their ever laying a hand
upon her. No sign of the wild woman was seen for
several months afterward.

At length, the wild woman returned, though her tactics
changed a bit. She continued to visit the potato fields
but became more bold and started entering the cabins
of the settlers on her visits. The settlers thought that
this must be a sign of desperation as she was risking
her life by entering homesteads at night while the
occupants slept. In addition to owning firearms, nearly
all the settlers kept two or more large and fiercely
protective dogs. The dogs were the alarm systems of
the day and were kept to protect the families from
interlopers be they man, big cat, bear, or something
else. The wild woman, seemingly, was able to step
right over these dogs and enter the premises.

This would seem to be an instance of disorientation or
paralysis by means of "zapping," a phenomenon that will be
covered in Part 4.

Once inside, she would take only what she needed. It was widely reported that she would tear a loaf of bread in two and take only one half. She would make off with a pitcher of cream and then, days or weeks later, return the pitcher, washed. She would steal tools – handsaws, hammers–polish them to a high luster and then surprisingly return them to their workbench.

Her most spectacular caper was swapping a feral piglet from the woods for a giant hog a farmer had fattened up.

All the while, nary a settler awoke during her intrusions nor did a dog so much as whimper upon her trespasses. This ability to sneak in and out of occupied homes gave rise to much superstition regarding just who, or what, the wild woman actually was. The slaves in particular were greatly disturbed at the prospect of receiving a nighttime visit from the wild woman and took to calling her "that thing that comes."

It was soon discovered that the wild woman would often enter a crib, or storage building, in the area that housed harvested corn. As always, she took only a trivial amount; but the curious felt this was just the way to catch her. All that need be done was have someone hide within the crib and shut the wild woman inside once she had entered. For several nights the watch was kept to no avail. The locals were not discouraged, however, and their patience was rewarded when the wild woman returned to the crib. The man on watch that night was lightly dozing when he heard the soft rustling of the cornhusks. All he needed to do was close the door, slide the bolt, and call out to his friends; however, he was overcome by an unexplainable dread and could not bring himself to stay even one more second inside the crib. He cried out in his fear before making his move and the creature tore out of the door with blinding speed. Another opportunity had been lost.

All of this had been going on for roughly eight years
when a crude camp was found in the heavily wooded
area near the river. Many of the items that had come up
missing over the last year or so were found there. No
clothing was found and the only bedding was a pile of
moss and leaves. Once again, pity for this wretched
creature welled up within the hearts of the settlers.
How could they just leave this poor woman alone out
in the wilderness? It was resolved then and there that
this mystery had to be solved. A new plan was devised
by the locals that was more systematic and
sophisticated than previous plans to capture the wild
woman. A number of hunters would form extended
lines and drive through the woods with leashed hounds.
Other mounted men, lassos in hand, would take
"stands" outside the brush line in the hopes of roping
the woman once she had been flushed out of the woods
and onto the open prairie.

The plan was implemented without success several
times. The hunters got a break when a settler found
fresh sign of the wild woman and took up positions
that very night in the area. Their quarry was, indeed,
in the area. It is generally known that hounds bark, bay,
and cry in different ways depending on the animal
whose scent they are following. That night under a
bright moon, the hounds raised a cry that their owners
had never heard before. Shortly after the hounds were
on the track there came a rustling of brush near one of
the lasso men who was waiting outside the timberline.
Suddenly, there she was, the wild woman of the
Navidad. The creature sprinted out of the brush at an
amazing rate of speed. She was attempting to reach
another heavily wooded area several hundred yards
across the open prairie. The rider spurred his horse to
full speed in an attempt to catch the sprinting figure.
To his amazement, the rider had to push his mount to a
full gallop to get within range of the fleeing woman.
He pulled to within lasso range several times but each
time his horse, obviously afraid of this strange

creature, shied and his throws came up short. Within moments. the wild woman reached the safety of the woods and the chase was over.

The disappointed hunters regrouped and the rider who had pursued the wild woman gave his account. He had drawn close to her several times before his horse shied away and had gotten a good look. She had long hair, almost down to her feet, that flew behind her as she ran. She wore no clothing of any kind and was covered completely in short brown hair. The rider had not been able to get a very good look at her face as she only took a few frightened glances over her shoulder at him. The rider said that initially she had been carrying an object of some kind but had dropped it during the pursuit. The hunters spread out to look and found what was described as a club, roughly five feet long. (TexasCryptidHunter.blogspot.com)

Illustration by Linda S. Godfrey

PART 4

"I'VE BEEN ZAPPED!"
AN ELECTRIC CONNECTION?

24. Shocking New Clues: My Local Research, Continued

In the spring of 2017, I kept finding structural evidence in the micro forests behind my mother's house. One afternoon, I suddenly realized—duh!—that they are right beside an electric substation. I had already been developing a rough working theory that Sasquatch are somehow able to absorb, store, and manipulate electromagnetic energy. And now here I was face to face with apparent corroboration, multiple obvious structures and strong audio evidence within close range of this major human power source. See "In the Micro Forest 2," "In the Micro Forest 3," and "In the Micro Forest 4." Can this species actually tap into an electromagnetic field (EMF), or do they perhaps simply *resonate* with it, find it soothing or stimulating in an autistic sense or otherwise?

"In the Micro Forest 5" shows what I found in the woods beside an even larger substation, fourteen miles away from the first.

On June 17, our local online community bulletin board (Front Porch Forum) contained the following post:

> Our dogs started going crazy around 11pm Friday
> night. It woke us up. At first we thought it was one of
> our kids breathing really loudly from the room next to

ours. But with further investigating it was coming from outside. We could hear it moving throughout the forest behind our house. I can't even describe the sound. I want to say something was distressed. It was so loud! Then it slowly faded and echoed as it moved away.

We just moved here a year ago from the West. I've never in my life heard a sound like that. I'm now wide awake researching it. I'm hoping that someone else heard it and knows what it is.

Of course, I wrote to her immediately, asking for details, but I never got a reply. Google Earth did not disappoint, however; this woman's home address turned out to border another micro forest less than half a mile from my mother's. And what do you suppose dominated the abutting field? An extensive solar power array.

What I found just within the tree line here seemed too good to be true, as I concede in "In the Micro Forest 7."

These tee-pees, huts, stacks, and wedgings could certainly have been produced, say, by children at a summer camp—public trails run through these woods—but deeper in, more heavy-duty structures could not have, especially this one below; the main cross-piece is an upside-down tree trunk, a foot in diameter, that rises sixteen feet into the air.

A short distance from the solar panel forest, I found several more remarkable structures much like those above, but this time hidden away on private property. This striking resemblance, far from public trails, sharply reduced my suspicion that the earlier examples were the work of kids.

The strangest construction in this spot was woven together above ground where, apparently, a human tree house had once been intended. The nailed ladder rungs remain, and several of the lower limbs have been sawn off. But instead of a platform made of lumber, there is an elaborate hodgepodge of peeled branches, all somehow staying aloft by some clever weave, like loose wicker, the whole thing aided in a few spots by thicker supporting beams standing on the ground. See this curiosity here: "In the Micro Forest 11: A Fake Tree House?"

In this one small area—containing the "tree house" and the two t-pee formations—I found excellent instances, too, of what I'm calling *lateral corroboration* or *side hustles*: slighter miniature versions, beside the main structures, of the very same design features. Yes, human beings could surely have fashioned a t-pee for fun but would be exceedingly unlikely to make sketchier replicas on the side. One can more easily imagine Sasquatch children practicing their craft beside the adult builders.

Photos by Rick Reles

In the picture below, #1 is beside the solar panel array, #2 is where I took the last four images, above, and #3 featured yet another structure, tucked away in another secluded corner of the city-side woods, half a mile from #2. See "In the Micro Forest 12."

All told, I had now located clear evidence in five different micro forests, all within three miles of one another, and all hugging neighborhoods and main arteries of our capital city. E^1 marks the electric substation just below my mother's house and the connected forests that are riddled with structures, and E^2 the large solar power array near the home of the woman who posted that panicked description of her unknown forest visitor.

I explored two *macro* forests as well—you can see them stretching out to the left, below—in order to compare notes with other researchers. Many have been finding that when there is a large tract of undeveloped forest beside a town or city, with abundant room for structures, they tend to appear instead at the *margins*.

For hours, I searched for evidence uphill, away from roads and houses, but my only success came downhill, where I've drawn the dotted lines. See "The Edge Preference: Sasquatch Structures Cluster Close to Town."

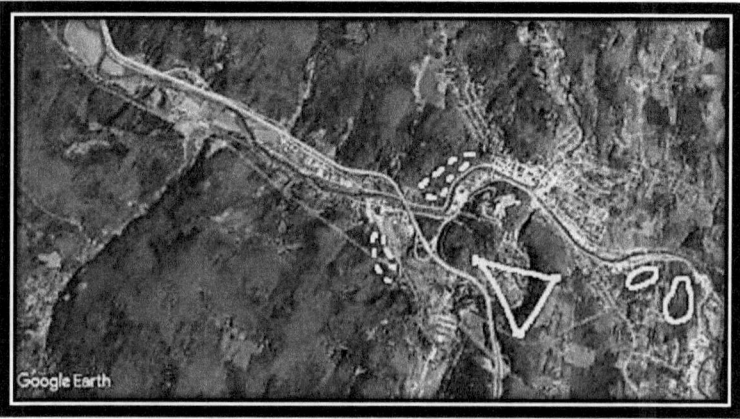

Are they marking the boundary of their territory? Are they establishing their kind of building as a direct counterpart to our own, as if saying, "We see your work...here's ours"? Or are they pushing their dominion up against ours as far as possible in order to assert power, to grab as much land as they can, and to try to prevent us from expanding our "footprint"?

Conversely, it seems that in the case of micro forests, bounded on all sides by civilization, structures are built in the more secluded pockets. The one exception is under the influence of human power sources, which tend to attract Sasquatch activity; for instance, #1 above features micro forest constructions just inside the tree line, a few yards from the solar power array.

Speaking of which, the last mind-boggling confirmation of this research season that I'd like to share with you occurred when I took my daughter to a summer music camp in Burlington, thirty-eight miles away, Vermont's largest city at 42,000. As soon as I pulled into the driveway of the host school, I had to slap my head and laugh: Here was yet another solar power array set beside a micro forest. While she practiced drums all day with her bandmates, I explored this startling prize. See what I found and hear the blatant percussion I recorded that night in "Sasquatch & Serendipity: How Three Lucky Breaks Taught me Where to Find Them."

25. Power Lines: A Well-Established "Hotspot"

For decades, researchers have consistently reported Sasquatch activity—knocks, vocals, structures, encounters—in and near power line corridors. A current example can be found in northern Massachusetts, where a woman calling herself Lady in Waiting has posted for years on YouTube channel bigfootresearch. Here are the titles I'd recommend.

- "Powerline Marathon" (steps/breathing)
- "Crashes, Knocks, Bops"
- "Cabin Structure Revisited"
- "Strange Artifacts"
- "Honeypot Howls"
- "My Howler Wood Knocks"
- "Possible Handiwork" (beneath power line)

11:57

I am certainly not suggesting that Sasquatch operate only near sources of electromagnetic radiation—not at all—but rather that where such power sources abut forests, even micro forests, they are likely to operate.

This hypothesis will, of course, need to be corroborated by other researchers.

In this connection, another interesting video is "Maryland Bigfoot World Found 4k," in which Marc Abell of Colorado Bigfoot travels 1700 miles due east to find, with a local researcher, many structures right beside a large power line.

I have a hunch that Sasquatch are able, somehow, to harvest electromagnetic energy from the environment (including the manmade environment), store it, and then wield it for a variety of purposes. I am proposing a concept akin to the unified field theory long sought by physicists; what this would mean in the context of Sasquatch research is a way to account for all of the most enigmatic capacities of the species under one principle.

What follows is excerpted from my 2016 eBook, *Electric Sasquatch: How a Natural Force May Explain "Supernatural" Powers.*

26. Getting "Zapped"

> I was walking in the woods at a habituation site and felt a pain high on my leg. I reached into my pocket and pulled out a 9-volt battery that had suddenly become scorching hot. I couldn't even hold it. (David Ellis, The Olympic Project)

Right at dusk, on March 27, 2012, I followed Florida researcher J.P. Smith to a spot where he'd recently seen a Sasquatch. As we were photographing a particularly interesting tree twist in the middle of a field, we heard a loud, clear yell from inside the tree line. At first, it sounded like a guy (a *human* guy) starting to shout "Heyyyyy," but then it quickly morphed into a sustained call, more like a howl.

After collecting our wits, J.P. and I headed carefully in that direction. At the corner of the field, not far from the apparent source of the vocalization, stood a really majestic oak tree with Spanish moss hanging from its limbs, forming a kind of room. When we were about forty feet away, J.P. noticed a shadow quickly shifting inside that room. He whispered, "I see something moving under there."

The atmosphere turned electric. We continued slowly forward, determined to get a better look. When we were only fifteen or twenty feet from the oak tree, J.P. went down on one knee, though I didn't know it because he was a couple steps behind me. (He later told me he'd just been "hit" with weakness and nausea.) At the same moment, I felt something I'd never felt before—a sizzling or sparkling sensation on my chest. It stopped me in my tracks and immediately drained all desire I'd had to get any closer to whatever was under that tree.

Without delay, we apologized for our disrespect and beat a hasty retreat.

See the event documented in the video "Encounter at the Old Oak Tree."

For many years, the research community has referred to such experiences as being "zapped" by Sasquatch and chalked them up to the effect of "infrasound"—powerful pulses or waves of sound beneath the range of human hearing. I have confidently passed along this explanation myself; after all, other large mammals use infrasound as well, elephants and whales to communicate over great distances, tigers and lions to disable prey. Our military has developed weapons that can strike enemy ranks with this same powerful form of energy, causing nausea, extreme weakness, paralysis, vertigo, disorientation, fear, and dread—the very symptoms so often reported by Sasquatch field researchers.

But now I'm not so sure. The more I think about it, the more I wonder what form of energy we're really talking about here. What I experienced beside the oak tree felt like electricity, not a sound wave; though I have never, to my knowledge, experienced the latter, nowhere can I find an association between infrasound and the sort of sparkly, sizzling sensation on the skin that I felt. It's easy, however, to learn from the Internet that receiving a mild to moderate electric shock often causes the same suite of disabling symptoms mentioned above.

Another witness describes her electrical experience, falling back on the unexamined term "infrasound." In my book *Sasquatch Rising 2013*, I quote from Rita, a BFRO Investigator who visited a North Carolina habituation site in December of 2007.

> One of the more profound experiences I had that afternoon was getting "zapped." This was over on the other side of [the homeowner's] yard, where [the Sasquatch are] not so friendly. All of a sudden I felt nervous. I felt a little nauseated, and my head was bothering me. I felt very unwelcome.
>
> [The homeowner and I] walked a little ways further down and ended up with some very thick brush

between us and the barn so we could not see the barn.
And we're poking around, trying to take pictures, and
all of a sudden we hear this THUNK! up at the barn,
and we're like, *What was that?* And then we hear it
again. I walked up there, with my video function on
my camera running, and didn't see anything, anything
that I *remember*, because once I got over there and I
turned off my video camera I got an infrasound
experience. It's like when you're about to put your
hand on a TV screen and you get that tingling all over
the surface of your hand. It was like that all over my
whole body, and worse on my arms and legs. And I
said something to her about it, and then I stepped
backwards.

In my mind, it only took two seconds. But she
informed me later, "Oh no, you were frozen and staring
straight ahead for about twenty seconds." And…I
didn't take her seriously, but I happened to have an
audio recorder in my hand, so I played it back and you
could tell by the beep when I turned off the video
function on my camera, and when I spoke to her, and
then you hear when I finally step backwards. It was a
total of thirty-six seconds.

Evidently, Mark Zaskey, Rita, and I did not experience sound
waves.

27. The "Bigfoot Curse"

In "Bigfoot and Electronic Interference," Nick Redfern writes about a typical phenomenon experienced by Sasquatch field researchers.

> Although we had tested all of our electronic equipment the night before, had charged up batteries where necessary, and had even put new batteries in all of our equipment that needed them, practically without exception all of our new equipment failed. The laptop battery… lasted just three minutes before failing. The batteries in our tape recorders also failed. It seems certain that there was some strange electromagnetic phenomenon at work here. (mysteriousuniverse.org)

Nearly every researcher can share similar accounts of what, for lack of any concrete explanation, has come to be known as "the Bigfoot Curse."

Here is another example among hundreds but one that was, remarkably, captured on video in real time. In his "Bigfoot Researcher's Journal" of January 2, 2016, Florida researcher Mark Zaskey and his partner Melanie are out at night in an area where Zaskey had a daylight sighting two years earlier. The voiceover explains that just as they begin hearing sticks snapping and then bipedal running, "His camera started acting up, and he felt like he had some type of electricity flowing through him. He got nauseous and panicked like he'd never felt before."

Such experiences have been reported hundreds of times, but rarely have they been clearly documented.

Watch the event unfold in "Episode of Sasquatch Electricity 1."

The apparent electric charge, hitting the camera, distorts the image and causes an audible buzzing

This past summer, Marc Abell (Colorado Bigfoot) experienced a very similar EMF ambush, but in this instance, it took place while he was trying to film a Sasquatch peeking from behind a tree sixty feet away. See "Episode of Sasquatch Electricity 2."

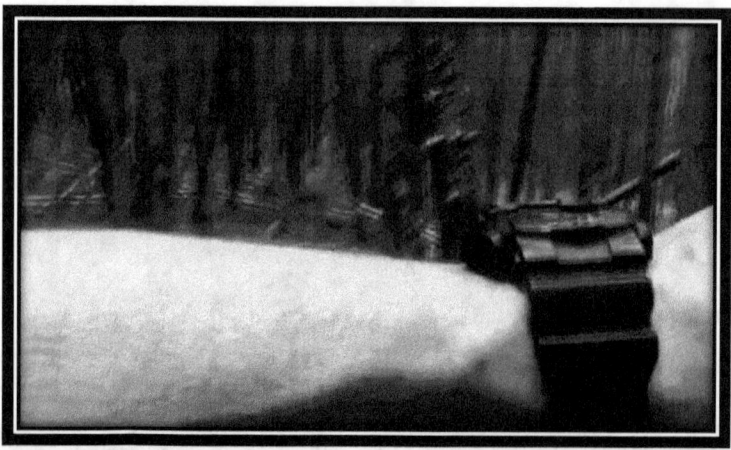

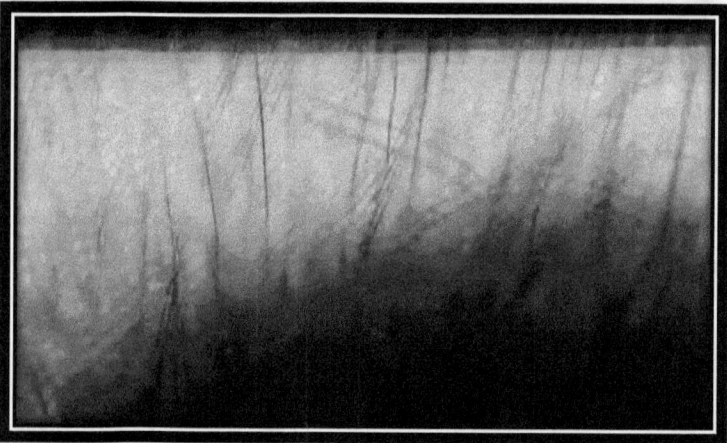

Shortly before the encounter, the hairs on Marc's arms stand up even though, as he says on the video, "I'm not scared." He felt "energy surging through my body."

Marc's camera image goes from normal to frozen during his sighting. This happens twice, each time he points the camera toward the subject. It is a brand new camera that has never malfunctioned before or since.

While infrasound and electromagnetic flow cause parallel cognitive and bodily symptoms, only electricity is capable of directly disrupting electronic equipment like this.

It's quite possible, too, that Sasquatch's uncanny ability to avoid camera traps stems from their intimate relationship with electromagnetic fields; they can likely "read" their environment through such fields and identify disturbances caused by charge-throwing equipment. (See the entry under "Electroreception" in the *Encyclopedia Britannica* at britannica.org.)

28. Targeting

As the years—and now decades—have passed during which Sasquatch researchers have regularly banded together for expeditions, going out at night into "active" areas, the accounts of zapping have steadily accumulated. While in most cases, two or more in the group will feel the effects, in a significant subset of cases, just *one* of them will be struck down with strong symptoms, the others remaining entirely unaffected, even though they were all standing or sitting in close proximity.

I have witnessed this precise targeting myself. In November of 2007, I joined my friend Michael Greene in North Carolina's Uwharrie National Forest, the site where, nineteenth months later, he would shoot his well-known thermal footage; see "Clips from the Michael Greene Thermal Footage."

After midnight, scanning through his thermal vision scope, he spotted the shape of a massive figure, like a tall football player with shoulder pads, walking among the trees at about seventy feet. He turned his upper body toward me and the others, said, "Our friend is here," then took a moment to switch on the record function (limited battery life prevents him from recording constantly). When he turned back toward the trees, the figure had already receded from view. Michael was despondent. A veteran North Carolina tracker, sitting with us, commented, "Them buggers is slick." The thermal scope resembles a gun.

Earlier that same night, our youngest North Carolina Expedition member, the fifteen-year-old daughter of an attending couple, had the traumatic experience of being "zapped." She had been with her family at a neighboring campsite, sitting near the campfire, fifteen feet from the edge of the woods, pretty relaxed, when suddenly she was overcome with anxiety, felt nauseated and weak, with an intense pins-and-needles sensation in her arms. Her parents helped her walk over to join the rest of us. It was a warm night but she felt very cold; I brought her a blanket from my car.

Although they were sitting right beside her at the fire, neither her father nor her mother suffered the slightest symptoms of having been "hit." Was this child selected because she was the youngest and most vulnerable in her small group?

Regardless of the reason behind this apparent targeting, the question arises, How is such a choice even possible? What kind of energy is being employed? Once again, the answer seems to lie in the direction of electricity rather than sound. Let's take a brief look at the physics behind these two options.

Sound is a wave of pressure or compression (a mechanical wave). Hence, it requires a medium to propagate through. With distance, moving through air and facing resistance, sound waves spread out and their energy quickly dissipates.

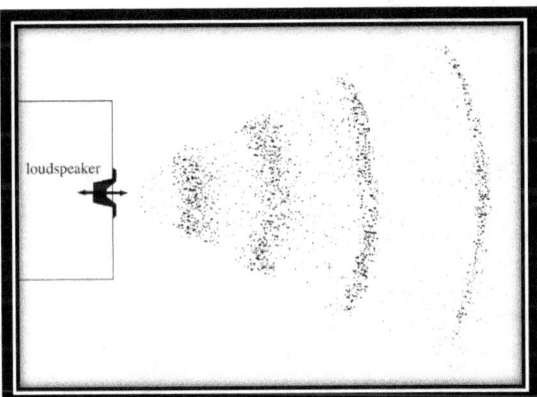

Electromagnetic waves, on the other hand, do not spread so broadly so near to their source, and this is for two reasons:

1. They require no medium to propagate through (they can travel across the vacuum of space as readily as across our terrestrial atmosphere), which means that they suffer no resistance as they travel through the air,

whereas in the case of a mechanical force such as a
sound wave, it's resistance that acts to "flatten it out,"
as when you're spraying a garden hose into the wind.

2. Instead of traveling at the speed of sound,
electromagnetic waves travel at the speed of light
(because they belong to the light spectrum), which is
nearly 900,000 times faster; therefore, as they cross a
distance of, say, one or two hundred feet, they barely
have time or room to spread out before striking their
target—if, that is, they are being purposefully *directed*
or *focused*, which certainly matches reported
experience.

But couldn't sound waves be focused as well? Yes, but with a
crucial limitation. In all types of energy waves, high frequencies
(short wavelengths) are far more conducive to the formation of
focused beams than are low frequencies (long wavelengths).
Infrasound (with its long wavelengths) is an extremely poor

candidate for beam formation. As is made clear in "Direction Loudspeakers" (explainthatstuff.com), sound waves are routinely focused into beams, but only at high frequencies. This is why ultrasound, not infrasound, is used as a diagnostic tool in medicine; it can be trained into concentrated beams that can probe the body and interact with tissue structures to create images.

In other words, if we suspected Sasquatch of using ultrasound (like bats or dolphins), rather than infrasound (like elephants, whales, or lions), we could plausibly propose that it is this kind of energy that they use to pick us off surgically, one by one. Unfortunately, this suspicion does not fit the requirements of the case, simply because ultrasound does not produce the symptoms associated with being "zapped"; again, its ability to pass through our bodies without causing damage is exactly what qualifies it for safe clinical applications.

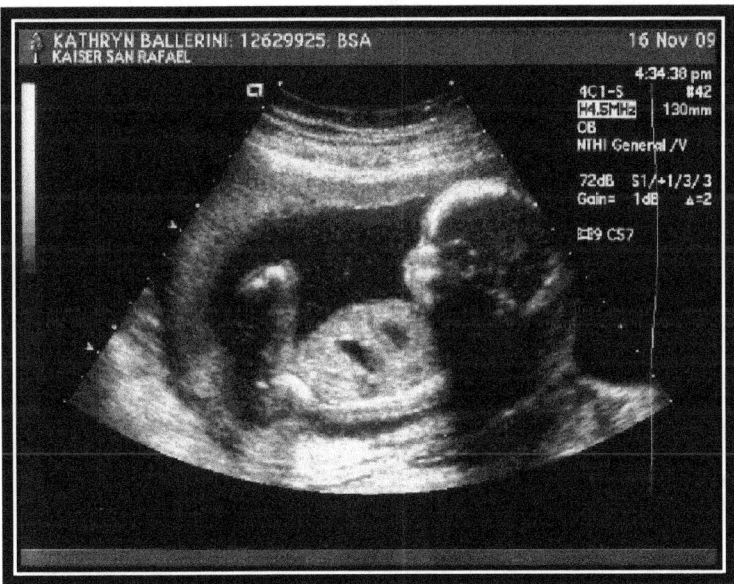

Electromagnetic frequencies are hundreds of times higher than infrasonic frequencies, which leads us, once again, to finger the former as our culprit. At this early point in our understanding of the species, who knows how Sasquatch are able to generate, aim, and deliver these beams of energy at human interlopers? Yet, they seem to have somehow adapted this faculty.

29. Eye Glow

For years, witnesses have reported seeing large double discs of colored light—yellow, amber, white, red, green, blue—among the trees at night, in association with stick breaks, tree pushes, wood knocks, whoops, bipedal footsteps, and other Sasquatch sounds. Many attributed this effect to light reflecting off the *tapetum lucidum*, a layer of retinal cells in nocturnal creatures that causes their eyes to shine at night when illuminated. Not wishing to partake of a supernatural-seeming explanation, researchers long resisted the notion that this light could be anything other than the result of reflection from an external source. But eventually, the weight of anecdotal evidence—countless reports of glowing eyes in the midst of pitch dark—piled up to the point at which no serious observer can now continue to deny the plain fact that Sasquatch eyes *do emit* light.

Researcher Pat Rance filmed in the back yard of an Oklahoma habituation site; see "Oklahoma Eye Glow 2007." And here is an analysis of a video apparently showing a Sasquatch at a window, its eyes glowing too: "Bigfoot Caught Looking Through Window (ThinkerThunker)."

But how is such a thing even possible? Noting an apparent similarity between this phenomenon and that of *bioluminescence*—the light produced by fireflies, some fungi, and many marine creatures—has led many to presume that something similar must be going on within the eyes of Sasquatch.

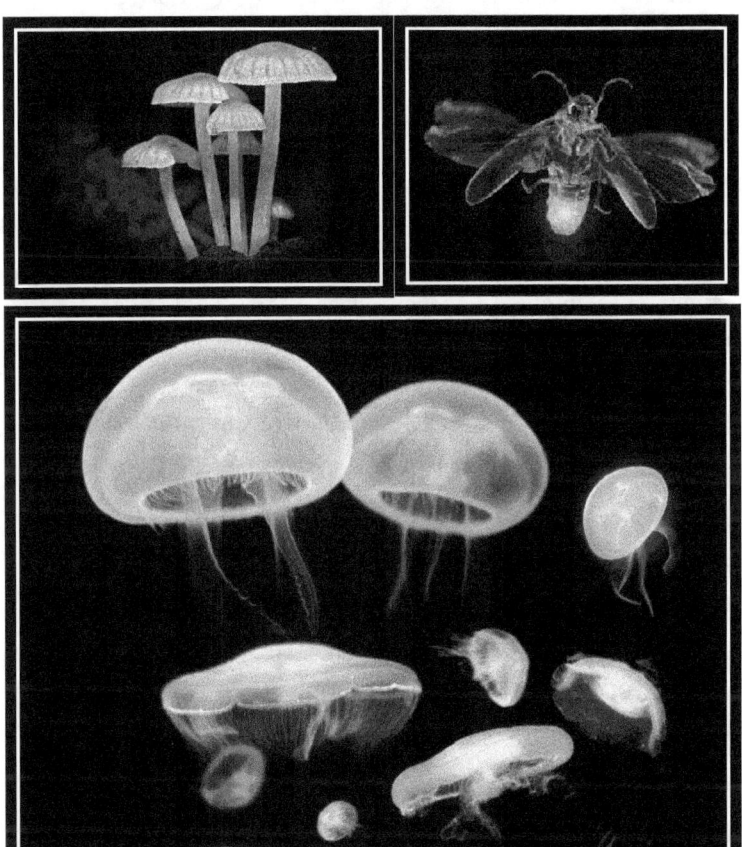

I'd like to suggest an alternative explanation. If it's true that this species is able to generate and control some kind of electrical charge, it would seem likely that their eye glow relates to this trait rather than to a non-electric chemical reaction. Why include two separate and very different forms of energy production when just one can do the job? Under the concept of Occam's razor, a theory should seek to pare down the number of separate assumptions needed to account for the empirical evidence.

Furthermore, based on numerous field reports, Sasquatch seem able to adjust their eye glow at will, changing colors, increasing or decreasing its intensity, even turning it off entirely. From an evolutionary standpoint, this only makes sense; if this light were the result of a chemical reaction that operated automatically and constantly (or worse, blinking like a lightning bug) as in bioluminescent organisms, this would pose a major problem, causing Sasquatch to be involuntarily lit, severely impairing their ability to hide when they need to, to "disappear" under the cloak of darkness.

Much more logically, for purposes of survival, their eyes would, under favorable conditions, send out light beams, to help them see and to intimidate the opposition. This ability would explain a commonplace perception reported by witnesses, the distinct sensation of "being stared at" that leads so many to vacate the area or else to turn and spot an enormous observer.

According to Dr. Colin Ross, in the video "Patent Approved for Eyebeam Detection Device," human beings, too, emit an "eye beam," though at a very low energy level, far lower than what Sasquatch must reach. We can often correctly sense when we're being looked at from across a room, even given our comparatively feeble electromagnetic signals. How much would our evolution have had to boost or alter this emission for our own beams of attention to enter the visible spectrum?

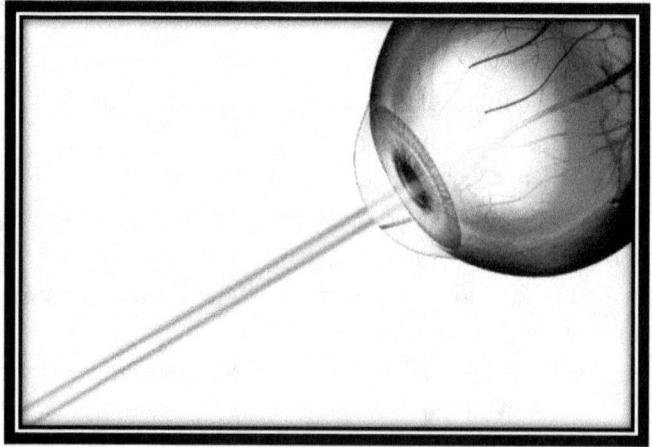

I think that Sasquatch eye glow is electrical in nature, like the other allegedly "supernatural" phenomena associated with this species.

30. Flashes of Light and "Orbs"

This is a hotly contested issue within the research community. Some have seen these strange manifestations in association with Sasquatch; others doubt the credibility or sanity of those who have. Some attribute these lights to ghostly or extraterrestrial influences; others laugh at such beliefs.

A woman I have known for years and come to trust entirely, who goes by No-Bite in my books *Sasquatch Rising 2013* and *Our Life with Bigfoot*, has on several occasions watched illuminated spheres moving through the trees beside her East Texas home. One night, one of these balls of light seemed, she said, "to be patrolling my property in a square grid." No-Bite grabbed her sawed-off shotgun and unloaded on this object. "The thing went dark and a whole lot of branches and leaves came raining down."

On the April 7, 2016, episode of "Finding Bigfoot," Ranae and Bobo spot two small orbs at night in Oregon's Klamath Reservation, and in a recent article, "A Case for Infrasound," Cliff Barackman takes such accounts seriously. He is one of the most level-headed and intelligent observers on the scene, though his conjecture here remains rooted in the acoustical paradigm.

> Considering that infrasound can cause visual hallucinations, it doesn't seem unreasonable to suggest that this could be part of the reason that strange lights are sometimes included in Sasquatch reports. (cliffbarackman.com)

Barackman is correct. NASA report #19770013810 puts the resonant frequency for the human eye at 18 hertz and explains that under the influence of infrasound, which operates at a much lower frequency, the eyeball would vibrate, causing a significant "smearing" of vision.

As children, we've all discovered that pushing on our eyes through closed lids can give us a fantastic light show, so probably assaulting the eyeball with soundwaves, too, can produce a similar effect.

And yet, first of all, both infrasound and electricity cause vibration, so any explanation that relies upon this factor can apply to both types of energy.

Second, in order to perceive a continuously unfolding phenomenon, such as No-Bite's traveling ball of light and many others' similarly uninterrupted "visions," a witness would need to be subjected to an unwavering dose of infrasound *or* electricity at a sustained level and lasting for several minutes, causing a smoothly ongoing hallucination, which seems a highly unlikely scenario.

Third, therefore, such displays are more coherently understood as being objectively real, external occurrences, especially when we consider that these episodes often involve several witnesses, who all report seeing the same thing.

One prominent example among many comes from the site of the famous Berry/Morehead Sasquatch recordings of the early 1970s, obtained in the Sierra Nevadas of California. To learn the story behind this historic audio evidence, see "Sasquatch Language 1: Scott Nelson and Ron Morehead Interviewed August 15, 2011" and Sasquatch Language 2: Scott Nelson Interviewed January 18, 2012."

These articulate vocalizations—generally accepted as authentic, non-human, and amounting to *speech* in the purest sense of the term—are now firmly lodged in the ears of all informed researchers, but one vivid aspect of the original experience has remained little known.

In their 1976 book *Bigfoot*, B. Ann Slate and Alan Berry chronicle several participants' very unusual observations.

"Well, there's something funny going on," said Lewis, "because there was a bright flash from up there that just lit up the whole area."

As both Warren and his son emerged from the shelter, there was another "flash." "I was looking right at it," Warren said. "It was like a strobe light, it lit up the whole camp scene."

He said it seemed to have come from about fifteen feet above ground and about thirty feet away, in the trees…. To me, it seemed like the light source was round and ball-like, maybe two to three feet in diameter, and it had a bluish cast…. At first, we thought it might be static electricity, because we didn't move very much while we watched. Mostly, we just stood still. But when we began to move around, we found out that the more we moved, the faster the flashes came."

In one experiment, he and Lewis walked to a clearing uphill, leaving Larry and David at the shelter to watch the effects. "We wanted to see if the lights would follow us," Warren said. And the lights did follow them, it seems, exploding every so often in different locations overhead. Larry saw one of them just as it went off. The light seemed to come from something bright about the size of a basketball, he said.

This description closely matches that of "lightning balls" (aka "ball lightning"), an atmospheric phenomenon that has been noted through history but not yet satisfactorily explained by science. In *The Electric Shock Book*, Oxford University lecturer and don Michael Shallis writes that

Lightning balls are glowing spheres that move freely through the air, sometimes penetrating walls. The balls generally are between an inch and up to a few feet in diameter. Normally yellow, red, or white, the balls sometimes glow purple or even green and not infrequently change colour as they probe their way through the atmosphere. The glowing ball may glide silently along or act as if it is inquisitive, searching the space around it as if it had an intelligence of its own. The balls may be accompanied by a hissing sound. The amount of energy required for the emission of light from such glowing spheres would generate enough heat to cause damage or injury, yet we find accounts of ball lightning where no heat seems to be emitted by the ball. There is no obvious answer in conventional physics.

That last statement notwithstanding, researchers have had no reason to believe that lightning balls are anything other than a natural occurrence having to do with a form of electrical or electromagnetic energy—that is, energy manifesting in the outside world, rather than as some trick of perception.

This curious "behavior" of seeming to follow people may relate to Coulomb's Law, a law of physics describing the electrostatic interaction between electrically charged particles or, on a larger scale, between electrically charged objects. The law was first published in 1785 by French physicist Charles Augustin de Coulomb and was essential to the development of the theory of electromagnetism. This interaction is a *non-contact* force that acts over some distance of separation. Think of how a charged balloon will pull toward one's skin or how, after we comb our hair, the comb will suddenly attract pieces of paper.

The two objects need to possess opposite charges in order for this law to apply, which is not difficult to contemplate; if the "orbs" are positively charged, like the balloon in the example, they might move toward people, who are normally negatively charged.

On the one hand, it seems clear that there exists some kind of energetic relationship at play, because the men were followed at times and, at others, "we found out that the more we moved, the faster the flashes came."

On the other hand, though, if what was on display here were Coulomb's Law alone, why would the spheres not simply bump right into the men, as do charged balloons, and perhaps with disastrous results?

My view is that these concentrated doses of airborne energy associated with Sasquatch are being produced by the primates themselves, who are then able to *control* them by means of their own energetic interaction, to wield them to their advantage, maybe to steal from their opponents the benefit of stealth: "It was like a strobe light, it lit up the whole camp scene." Flooding people or animals with light would confer the added bonus of sharply diminishing their night vision, rendering the Sasquatch even more securely hidden within the surrounding darkness.

31. "Invisibility Cloaking" and "Portals"?

Here is another highly controversial topic. Some researchers of a mystical turn of mind have become convinced that Sasquatch are "interdimensional beings." Some even claim to have witnessed them stepping through an apparent doorway or "portal," emerging from another dimension and entering our own.

The trusted friend whom I mentioned above, the woman from East Texas, swears that she once saw a Sasquatch crossing the road in front of her car, in broad daylight, only to vanish right before her eyes. Many others report similar mind-boggling experiences.

The leading proponent of the supernatural explanation is Kewaunee Lapseritis, whose books *The Psychic Sasquatch* and *The Sasquatch People* describe interactions with invisible Sasquatch; sometimes, he can watch footprints still forming as the subject steps through the grass.

Invisibility cloaks being developed at the University of California (2015)

Not surprisingly, I think there's a much more this-worldly explanation available to us. Harry Potter-like invisibility cloaking technology is becoming mainstream science. As shown in this "The Optics of Invisibility" (YouTube channel GallowaySarah), in order to make an object no longer visible, it is necessary to bend or channel light around it in such a way that what the viewer sees is what stands behind the object rather than the object itself; this gives the clear impression of being able to see *through* it.

Yes, such distortion of ordinary vision is a high bar to set for an evolutionary adaptation, yet nature is rich with breathtaking examples of camouflage, of fool-proof blending into the environment. To me, the capacity to execute an optical illusion of this nature is far more readily acceptable than the notion of literal, physical disappearance.

But what does this preternatural parlor trick have to do with electricity? It turns out that, remarkably, invisibility can be contrived by means of "metamaterials" even more effectively than through hand-held cloaks; all it takes is the right kind of electromagnetic field.

> Metamaterial cloaking, based on *transformation optics*, describes the process of shielding something from view by controlling electromagnetic radiation. Objects in the defined location are still present, but incident waves are guided around them without being affected by the object itself. This discovery was published in the journal *Science* in 2006. (Wikipedia.com)

One can well envision a Sasquatch encounter in which the human observer happens to witness a phase shift in the electromagnetic field. This would look for all the world as if the visitor or visitors were stepping into or stepping out of our dimension, crossing a threshold. Some witnesses even describe a glowing "doorway" or similar opening, such as would be formed by an electromagnetic corona surrounding an active process of "appearing" or "disappearing."

The fact that Kewaunee Lapseritis is able to see impacts in the physical world caused by his visitors—e.g., footprints proceeding through the grass—suggests that they are *still there*, albeit unseen; likewise, witnesses often hear heavy, bipedal footsteps right in front of them in the forest but search in vain for the cause, as in this account: "Cloaked Bigfoot Encounter (2013)" (YouTube channel Billingsgate Sasquatch).

The electromagnetic interpretation fits the evidence more tightly than a supernatural interpretation. If Sasquatch has the capacity to vanish at will—*really* vanish—then why are databases filled with tens of thousands of sightings throughout North America since the 1950s, and why did the figure in the Patterson/Gimlin Film not instantly exit into thin air as soon as she spotted Roger and Bob, rather than allowing herself to be filmed in exquisite detail?

Because it's not magic; it's physics and physiology.

32. Inducing Silence

A common experience right before a Sasquatch encounter is the abrupt falling silent of the forest. Crickets, katydids, etc., will hush all together. Why?

As we know, crickets, for example, respond to ground vibration and will stop chirping when a person or animal steps near. But after a short period, if the vibration ceases, they will resume their music. According to hundreds of reports, when a Sasquatch is on the scene, the ambient sounds do *not* resume, even if—after initially making his presence known—he stands stock still for a long time, as his kind are so adept at doing.

Which is more likely, that crickets, katydids, etc., are staying mum—like we do—because of fear, even in the absence of Sasquatch footsteps, or that they are reacting to atmospheric (electromagnetic) vibration continuing to emanate from the Sasquatch? Insects operate at a much too primitive level for the first option; they are not nudging one another and whispering, "Shh....*shhhhh!!* Pipe down! He's not gone yet!"

There is precious little research on the effect of electromagnetic fields on insects, though I was able to find a study out of Simon Fraser University, "The Effect of Electrostatic Stimuli on German cockroach Behaviour," in which the author presents

> evidence that electrical circuits modify the behaviour of several insects, attracting or arresting *Blattella germanica, Supella longipalpa, Lepisma saccharina, Thermobia domestica* and *Forficula auricularia*, and repelling *Periplaneta americana*. Based on extensive experimentation, it appears that primarily the electric component of electromagnetic fields contributes to the attraction and/or arrestment response.

For our purposes, of course, the response of most interest would be "arrestment"—paralysis.

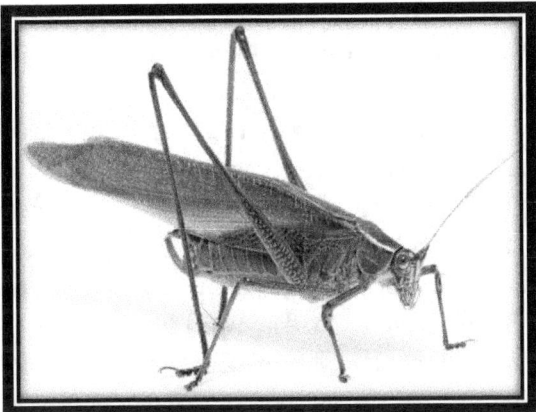

Texas bush katydid

33. Could it be Chi?

My friend and fellow researcher John Esposito has raised the possibility that the force Sasquatch is able to manipulate could be chi, or some version of it. From what I've been able to learn, this kind of energy may bear some relationship with electromagnetism; see the video "Ultra-Violet Bio-Energy Levels Measured in Chi Healer."

In traditional Chinese culture, chi is an active principle forming part of any living thing. The word literally translates as "breath" or "air" and figuratively as "material energy," "life force," or "energy flow." Chi is the central underlying principle in traditional Chinese medicine and martial arts.

Synonyms are found in many cultures, including (but not limited to) *prana* in India, *pneuma* in ancient Greece, mana in Hawaiian culture, *lüng* in Tibetan Buddhism, *manitou* in Native American Algonquian groups, *ruah* in Jewish culture, and *vital energy* in Western philosophy.

There is intriguing evidence that certain practitioners are able to direct their chi energy at distant objects, animals, and people. In the video "Chi Energy - master gets animals to sleep," the master claims that his power actually *increases* with distance.

Some claim to be able to form chi balls (or psi balls) between their hands, a feat that may relate to the spheres of light that people witness in association with Sasquatch. I haven't been able to find any proof that such balls can be made visible, but here is an introduction to the concept: "How to make a Psi Ball in 5 Minutes: Learn Psychic Telekinesis Training for Beginners."

Might Sasquatch be accomplishing something very similar but far more potently?

Recalling the so-called "electric people" phenomenon spotlighted earlier, we can speculate that such individuals may be gifted (or cursed) with an excess of chi energy, which is the cause of their chronic disruption of electronic devices. And this may, in turn, be the source of the same phenomenon so often experienced in the presence of Sasquatch.

See also "Qigong master projecting his chi energy" and "Chi Energy Documentary - Proof of Chi."

But how does chi relate to the electromagnetic spectrum? Many studies have established a connection. In the article "Measuring the Chi in Tai Chi," on Indiana University's website, Margaret Moga explains that

> Scientists have attempted to measure bioenergy, or chi, with varying success, using many different types of meters and instruments. Most promising have been the studies using voltmeters and magnetometers to measure the electrical and magnetic fields surrounding energy healers and Qigong practitioners. In Japan, Seto and colleagues (1992; 1996) recorded extremely large magnetic fields adjacent to the heads, bodies and hands of Qigong practitioners during breathing meditations and during external chi emission. Elmer Green and colleagues (1991) recorded surges in the electrostatic potential of healers during distant healing sessions at the Menninger Clinic in Kansas. In my laboratory in Terre Haute, Indiana, we have observed a distinct magnetic field waveform which appears with high frequency during energy healing sessions. (Indiana.edu)

34. Electricity Drawn from Where?

At first, I leaned toward the idea that they must be internally *generating* it through a process akin to that of various marine creatures, such as the electric eel. Most of this eel's body is filled with *electrocytes*, the cells that generate the electric charge. Electric eels contain several thousand of these cells, each with a negative and positive pole. They occur in a long chain, multiplying the charge as in a stack of batteries and producing up to 600 volts, which the animal can release from its head. This natural process may even have inspired the invention of the battery, since the analogy was already noted by Alessandro Volta himself.

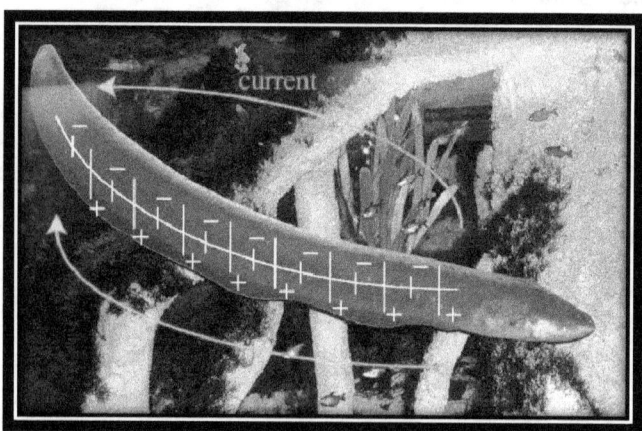

So I eagerly began searching for any terrestrial parallels but could locate none at all among mammals, much less among primates *per se*.

There are, however, certain *human beings* who are endowed with an extreme affinity to electricity, able to deliver a powerful shock—though they do not seem to create this energy themselves.

Returning to Michael Shallis's *The Electric Shock Book*, we find well-documented cases of so-called "electric people," for example that of Sheila, an otherwise ordinary woman living in Britain.

> Sheila all too easily becomes charged with static electricity. Almost everyone has blue flashes of static when removing pullovers in a dark room.... But Sheila's ability to build up large static charges on her body far outstrips these normal displays. She cannot touch her dog, when charged, for fear of hurting him. Two-inch-long sparks flash from her fingers when she reaches for a light switch. One of her three sons has inherited this high body static and the pair of them can exchange sparks and electrical flashes when close. The real trouble, however, comes with appliances. For example, she boiled the tropical fish when her hand accidentally touched the tank's thermostat; when she was ironing one day, there was a sudden and massive blue flash that threw her back against the kitchen wall; when she recovered, she found the whole base of the iron had blown out.

Shallis studied "more than sixty cases in Britain of people with symptoms similar to Sheila's, and the archives contain similar cases from the past."

> Even before we lived in an electric environment, cases were recorded. One such was reported in *The American Journal of Science* in 1838. It concerned a woman who produced one-and-a-half-inch sparks from her fingers over a six-week period, often at a rate of one every fifteen seconds. In several cases, the disturbance was activated by mood. One woman describes herself as "the person responsible for 'blowing' light bulbs" and goes on to say that when she is upset, up to half a dozen bulbs will go off. Emotional tension is certainly a thread that runs through many of the cases I have investigated.

I noticed an affinity between the mood-related quality of this electric build-up and discharge and the circumstances in which people tend to find themselves zapped—when they are encroaching into Sasquatch territory, no doubt causing stress and anger.

Further, reading this book sparked a memory of the famous 1895 encounter between E.S. Ingraham and an apparent Sasquatch. Ingraham was a well-respected explorer, mountaineer, and author, who founded the Seattle school system. Nowhere else in his writings does he touch upon this subject, only here; the rest are straight-ahead accounts of mountaineering adventures and essays on educational reform.

While descending into the steam-caves of a crater near the 14,411-foot summit of Mount Rainier, Ingraham became aware of "a peculiar sensation of the body, such as a person feels when standing upon an insulated pool with his hand holding the pole of an electrical machine slightly charged."

This is, of course, strikingly similar to what Rita experienced, 112 years later and diagonally across the continent, in North Carolina: "It's like when you're about to put your hand on a TV screen and you get that tingling all over the surface of your hand." And beside the Florida oak tree, when I got too close, I felt that sparkling, sizzling sensation on my chest.

Then, Ingraham caught sight of the creature.

> The crown of its head was pointed, with bristled hair pointing in every direction. The nails of its fingers and toes were long and pointed and resembled polished steel more than hardened cuticle. The palms of its hands and the soles of its feet were hard and calloused. In fact, the whole body, while human in shape, seemed very different in character from that of the human species.

Gradually, an electric glow covered the entire body with light-centers at the ends of those pointed nails, the eyes, and the top of the head. It began to rub its feet rapidly upon the floor of the cave.

This increased the glow of its body and caused the light-centers to shine with increased brilliancy. It seemed to receive some vital fluid from the earth that at once gave new vigor to its whole system.

This rapid rubbing of the feet is an especially interesting detail; it's just what we do when we want to build up static electricity from a carpet and then shock someone as a prank. But this individual was doing the same thing on a *rock* floor, not carpet. How could that produce static electricity?

The Mount Rainier crater and cave system that Ingraham explored is part of the Mount Rainier Volcano, which, though it looks quiet, it is still considered an active volcano, and there are frequent tremors here, sometimes occurring at a rate of one per day.

Earthquakes, even minor tremors, produce electricity, which rises up through the ground, especially when conducted by minerals in rock. According to M.J.S. Johnston of the US Geological Survey, "During the past few decades, we have seen a remarkable increase in the quality and quantity of electromagnetic data recorded before and after earthquakes."

In other areas with consistent seismic activity, too, electricity may be readily available underfoot, accounting for some "supernatural" observations. The article "Mystery of Earthquake Lights Traced to Electrical Charges in Rocks" explains that

> the strange phenomenon of earthquake lights—
> sometimes resembling bluish flames, lightning strikes,
> or floating orbs—seems to be associated with tiny
> crystal defects in certain rocks that can release electric
> charges, according to *National eographic*. Researchers
> examined the historical record of earthquake lights
> from around the world and detailed their latest findings
> in the journal *Seismological Research Letters*. Certain
> conductive rocks such as basalts and gabbros can be
> found in "dike" structures that formed as magma
> cooled in vertical faults reaching as deep as 97
> kilometers underground. (spectrum.ieee.org)

Earthquake lights are captured in this photo taken at Tagish Lake, in the Yukon Territory, 1972

I think that Sasquatch are able to take up and discharge electricity far more effectively than we can; moreover, we ourselves can do so far more effectively than is generally recognized. In an article called "The Body Electric," author and ecologist David Suzuki, PhD, writes that

> humans can absorb and emit electrical current, which can have more of an effect than you may imagine. People can attract and carry a current of static electricity, sometimes even resulting in a small explosion when something metal is touched. The release of a static charge can be so intense it can actually ignite the fumes of a poorly ventilated gas pump, which is why it is advisable to touch the side of your vehicle before beginning to put gas into your car.

> Carrying a charge of static electricity is so common that responsible electronic manufactures require their technicians to wear a grounding strap on their wrist connected to a grounding pole. This ensures the charge of current that may be temporarily residing in them

does not arbitrarily move to the electronics and cause damage or malfunctions. (skininc.com)

If my hypothesis is correct, what we'd need to suppose of Sasquatch is that they were able, during evolution, to select for and enhance this same capacity to acquire, hold, and deliver a charge—along the lines of human anomalies such as Sheila, though more advanced—as an enormously effective hunting tool and defense mechanism.

But how can such energy be formed into a beam and shot at a distance? The jury is still out on this question, though it does seem that static electricity is capable of being propagated through space. In November 2014, a man posted a video of himself walking through "a beam of static electricity" beside the Google building in London; we can see his hair actually lifting off his head, and his cell phone goes haywire; see "Crazy static electricity beam" (YouTube channel Strykekyte). Interestingly, we've all heard numerous eyewitness testimonies in which people in close proximity to Sasquatch describe the sensation of their hair standing on end, too, though they mean the tiny hairs at the back of their neck and on their forearms.

In a city like London, though, electricity flows abundantly, whereas out in the forest, far from the electrical grid, what could Sasquatch possibly tap into that is more reliably available than seismic energy? Recent recent findings have revealed that there's enough power in trees for University of Washington investigators to run an electronic circuit, according to results published in the *Institute of Electrical and Electronics Engineers' Transactions on Nanotechnology*. To extract electricity from trees and convert it into useful energy, researchers built a boost converter capable of picking up as little as a 20-millivolt output and storing it to produce a greater output.

> "As far as we know, this is the first peer-reviewed paper of someone powering something entirely by sticking electrodes into a tree," said co-author Babak

Parviz, a UW associate professor of electrical engineering.

The UW team successfully ran a circuit solely off tree power for the first time. "It's not exactly established where these voltages come from," Parviz conceded. "But there seems to be some signaling in trees, similar to what happens in the human body but with slower speed. I'm interested in applying our results as a way of investigating what the tree is doing." (Phy.org)

Whatever the tree is doing, Sasquatch seem able to act as a "boost converter" themselves, drawing up and storing electric energy from this source, gathering it from tree to tree in order to produce a cumulative output when needed.

Another likely source of energy—abundantly available during the past seventy years—is power lines, electric substations, and—available more recently—solar power arrays. Although this technology was not part of the evolutionary picture, it now pumps strong electromagnetic currents deep into North American forests, crossing even very remote stretches.

We still know so little, which leaves a wide berth for speculation. For instance, it may turn out that wood knocking helps in the uptake of charges from trees—or conversely, does this action *release* excess energy, serving as a means of regulating the carried load in the body?

The overarching question, of course, remains: How do these primates even harvest, hold, and then deploy this natural force at all?

PART 5

THE NEARNESS OF YOU
ANTHROPOLOGY IN A NEW KEY

35. Sasquatch Habitat is Shrinking!

This is a common misconception.

> Every day now, the world of the Sasquatch keeps getting
> smaller and smaller. Their habitat is large tracts of
> undeveloped wilderness. We have only to look around
> us to see the fact that this kind of living space is rapidly
> disappearing from the face of the North American
> continent. Unless this encroachment by man can be
> stopped, then the days of these creatures' existence are
> numbered, whether we ever prove that existence or not.
> (K. Steven Monk, georgiabigfootsociety.com)

Of those who are aware that the species often operates right
alongside human civilization, some try to use the "vanishing
habitat" fallacy to explain such a startling state of affairs: They are
being *forced* out of their natural homelands.

First of all, however, as we have seen, Sasquatch do not
require "large tracts of undeveloped wilderness"—quite the
contrary. Second, according to US Census records, 1926 was the
last year in which more people lived in rural areas than in urban
and suburban areas, and since then, our nation has seen a steady
flow away from the countryside and toward the cities. Combine
this with conservation efforts and the establishment of protected
state and federal forest land and we can readily understand how
there are vastly more trees in our country today than there were a
century ago. According to the Food and Agriculture Organization,
"Forest growth nationally has exceeded harvest since the 1940s."
The greatest gains have occurred in the eastern United States,
which was the region most heavily logged by European settlers
beginning in the 1600s.

For its part, Canada has more than one billion forested acres
and contains 10% of the world's timberland with more than 50%
of its land being tree covered. Fewer Canadian forests are affected

by logging each year.

Furthermore, our overall population is barely increasing anymore. An ongoing decline in the North American birth rate has led to a current yearly growth of less than 1%.

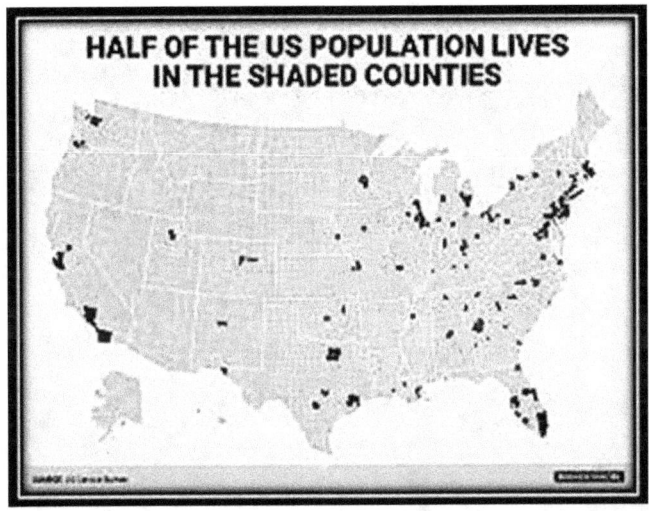

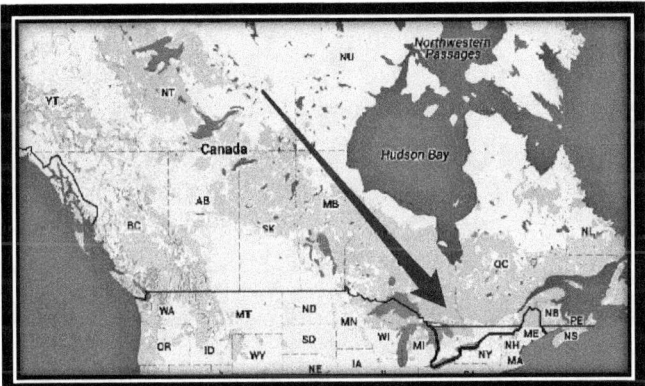

Half of Canada's population lives below this line.

Sasquatch has enjoyed untold thousands of years, before European colonization, to expand throughout these 9.5 million square miles, occupying every nook and cranny of suitable habitat. The million-dollar question, of course, is this: With all of the vast territory at their disposal, why do so many of them find it preferable to live alongside us?

36. Why a Stone's Throw Away?

I wish I had the answers, and I do mean the plural here; very likely, their persistent nearness is the result of a convergence of factors. I can offer my own personal top ten list of candidates, but I would love to hear others from you by email or in my Facebook group "The Sasquatch Listening Project."

1. Since we pose their greatest threat, some Sasquatch probably find it logical to monitor us and our routines as closely as possible; "keep your friends close and your enemies closer." See also Temple Grandin's concept of animals as being "curiously afraid"—that is, when sensing danger, they often feel less anxious when approaching the problem, checking it out, than when cowering at a distance. For the species in question, or at least a cross section of their population, this "checking out" process may simply be perpetual.

2. On the flip side, as *their* next of kin, we are probably compelling to them, so they gravitate toward us, not only at habituation sites (where they regularly make their presence known), but elsewhere as well (where they try not to). Thousands of accounts have confirmed that they tend to observe us—occasionally, we catch them doing so—and especially our children.

3. Their use of and affinity for electricity probably draws them to human sources in the form not only of substations and solar arrays but also of the electrical grid at large as it runs through homes, businesses, and neighborhoods.

4. As we ourselves know, there is a thrill in successful hiding, especially when the stakes are high. For a species many-fold more adept at hiding than we are, the thrill is probably many-fold greater.

5. To the extent that Sasquatch thought and behavior resemble those of our own autistic savants, they probably experience an increase in calm and control when fitting themselves into a known and finite space with known and finite rules. This is what autistic *Homo sapiens* are famous for doing. In the case of Sasquatch, sometimes this space is in the middle of nowhere (from our viewpoint), and sometimes it is smack in the middle of "our" territory. In the former circumstance, limbs, branches, trunks, and groomed earth form the boundaries up against which Sasquatch can lean, which is probably why they chop space up into manageable segments; recall the marked-off "perches," the "edging," "fencing," and "boxing" shown in "Appreciating Colorado Bigfoot 2: Sasquatch Home Spaces" and "Appreciating Colorado Bigfoot 3: Sasquatch Groundwork." (All serious Sasquatch field researchers find similar structuring of the environment.) In the latter circumstance, houses, streets, train tracks, power lines, etc., form the boundaries up against which they can lean, within which they can operate and attain control. And even in the case of such framed forests, surrounded by civilization, Sasquatch seek to further contour and subdivide; see my "In the Micro Forest" series.

6. To the extent, again, that autism is a useful lens through which to view this species, it would make sense that they enjoy using their keenest faculties in the pursuit of stability and authority. So do we, and autistic savants in

particular thrive on the mastery of informational systems; Daniel Tammet learned Icelandic in one week. For Sasquatch, too, the capacity to memorize, down to the most granular detail, our behavior patterns revolving around a micro forest—all the constants and variables within each local social system—would allow them to gain tactical and psychological leverage.

7. I suspect that Sasquatch are more territorial in such confined terrain than out in the wilderness—because they have to be. It's either stand firm or concede defeat. Whether they are recent arrivals to a given neighborhood forest or have lived here for centuries, they have a profound stake in the location now, and each square foot possesses a high premium. In other words, no matter what infrastructural development grows around or beside them, encroaching on their space, they are unlikely to be dislodged. No, of course, they do not continuously *reside* in every such patch of nature, but they certainly do renew their land claims regularly with fresh structures—like flags.

8. Whatever else they may be, they are also pranksters. What finer trick to play upon a smug and clueless crowd of stooges than secret infiltration?

9. This sense of control is probably heightened the closer to the Other they can push their envelope. In the dynamic contest between order and chaos, structure and entropy, each becomes more meaningful, more *itself*, when the two are starkly juxtaposed. For Sasquatch, maximum adjacency probably allows for maximum expression of identity, of style; if they can be simultaneously absent and "in our face," what a bold statement, an affirmation, an ultimate victory.

10. As ancient kin, we simply belong together, and for reasons that transcend logical analysis, a certain percentage of us, on both sides, will—like officially selected representatives—always embody and enact this truth in physical space. And fortunately, if we will only open ourselves to the available education, this dance can also more sharply define *us*, our gifts, our limitations, our place. As my friend at the East Texas habituation site has written, "These people fit in with us like gears. What we lack, these people possess. What these people lack, we possess."

I'd like to move now from the abstract to the very concrete with two how-to sections before we close, the first concerning what a new form of anthropology might look like, the second concerning how you as an individual researcher might best fit into this broader effort.

I would hope that our collective direction of travel will be toward less and less need for conjecture—like mine, above—and toward more and more demystification of the issues at hand as we empirically identify the logic behind Sasquatch behavior, point by point.

37. Anthropology in a New Key

For me, this phrase is not just a musical metaphor but also evokes the image of a key*hole*...with an ear listening in. I think our best bet in studying this species, in making significant progress toward understanding more about them, will be the widespread use of audio recording.

Because Sasquatch don't seem to mind ears.

They mind eyes.

More than a century ago, pioneers in the emerging field of anthropology helped nudge Western civilization out of its benighted, self-congratulatory worldview by shedding light on the phenomenon of diverse cultures. The breakthrough lay in successfully challenging the comfortable notion that people living in radically different ways from those of Europeans or Americans were "primitives" languishing on some lower rung of the ladder of human development.

Field work pioneer Margaret Mead among the Samoans (1925)

The parallel to our situation in 2018, and no doubt into the near future, is that now the entire human race itself—well, the 99%

who have remained in the dark concerning the true personhood of Sasquatch—has been caught out in the same falsely entitled posture as "advanced" societies of old. We are proud to call ourselves the only human species and will need to similarly awake from such a parochial slumber.

Franz Boas, considered the father of modern anthropology, first advanced the concept of "cultural relativism" that saw culture as a set of learned behaviors. In an 1883 letter, Boas wrote,

> I often ask myself what advantages our "good society" possesses over that of the 'savages' and find, the more I see of their customs, that we have no right to look down upon them, to blame them for their forms and superstitions which may seem ridiculous to us.

In the same expansive spirit, novelist Molly Gloss writes of Sasquatch,

> They inhabit these forests so comfortably and inconspicuously, are enough like us to have shrewdly escaped our notice…. Perhaps they are no lower animal at all, but an evolutionary advance—have grown beyond poor *Homo sapiens* and understand the world well enough that they have no need to construct a civilization upon it. (*Wild Life*)

The operative distinction here is between *culture* and *civilization*. Sasquatch do seem to have opted out of the latter approach to being-in-the-world, but not the former. It is indeed their cultural landscape—including behavior, language, and social structures—that we will seek to illuminate in the coming years. Traditional methodology is clearly off the table in the present case; no on-site embedding, immersion, interviewing, or direct observation is possible, given what we covered in Parts 2 and 3. Nor is long-distance video monitoring a meaningful part of the solution, even as rare glimpses may come along; again, see "The Daily Life of Sasquatch: Nine Glimpses."

Whereas *Homo sapiens*, even in the most far-flung locations on Earth, have, for better or worse, proven willing to stay put in stable societies beneath the anthropological lens, here we have, in Sasquatch, an exceedingly mobile and nomadic style of existence—a perpetually receding target—that seems to aggressively fragment itself, avoiding congregation; they make themselves scarce in disparate family groups and clan cells, each occupying its own territory or a rotating network of territories. For a vivid picture of this freewheeling game plan, see Utah Sasquatch's video "Why I Don't Pose a Threat to Sasquatch."

So where does this leave us? I think we need to recast the discipline—or our corner of it—from an anthropology of direct contact to an anthropology of indirect contact. How might this fresh brand of social science be construed and conducted? Our range of choice is quite narrow, thanks to Sasquatch nature itself; our data will reach us through some form of mediation.

Emulating SnowWhiteBigfoot, we could pursue object-based communication at habituation sites. My hesitation here is not because I doubt that genuine reality and personal meaning changes hands in the course of such dialogues—it's wonderful what intimacy blooms on porches and in back yards—but rather that there seems to be a self-limiting principle at work, a lack of breakthrough to some richer, more transparent form of Sasquatch disclosure than playful rearrangements, copy-cat gestures, and surprising pranks. Even the most successful such experiments retain a kind of closed-loop quality, a steady state of mutual acknowledgement and appreciation within settled limits that, instead of bridging the fundamental gap between our species, ultimately only serves to accentuate it. It's as though we are trying to speak with a foreigner who stubbornly declines to learn our language, just as we remain—helplessly—ignorant of theirs.

Or *are* we helpless? This brings us back to audio recording.

38. Sasquatch Language

R. Scott Nelson, US Navy cryptolinguist (retired)

"By accident, one night in 2008," Scott Nelson recalls, "I stumbled onto what we think is a pretty big discovery. My eleven-year-old son wanted a subject for a school paper, so we're Googling 'Bigfoot Sounds,' and found the BFRO website, and I clicked on 'Samurai Chatter.' Of course, I was curious, since I'm a linguist: What are they talking about with 'chatter'? Almost immediately, I recognized this as having characteristics of language. And you know, I'm sure I would have passed over it just like any average guy if it had not been for the thousands of hours that I spent in the Navy speeding voice communications up, and slowing them down, and analyzing them for every characteristic that we could retrieve. It would have sounded to me just like apes fighting, like it's been described to me a hundred times since. Until you put it on a transcription program and retrieve those sounds off of there, you don't perceive the sounds. They're simply too fast. In fact, they're so fast, and the conversational turns that the creatures execute are so quick that they're virtually stepping on each other. So, I listened the first time through, and my son saw the look on my face, and he said, 'What? What is it, Dad?' And I said, 'Hold on.' And I played it over and I played it over, and there were very few, limited samplings of sound on the website. But I recognized language, and I said, 'Stevie, this is language. This is not human, I can tell, 'cause I don't know how many hundreds of humans I've listened to for hours on tape, and these are not humans. Yet, they're speaking a language."

One can hear audio samples at BigfootSounds.com. Also, listen on "Sasquatch Vocalizations: Clips from the Berry/Morehead Recordings"; "Sasquatch Language 1: Scott Nelson and Ron Morehead Interviewed August 15th, 2011"; and "Sasquatch Language 2: Scott Nelson Interviewed January 18th, 2012."

Thirty-six years earlier, in 1972, at an isolated deer camp in the High Sierra Mountains of Eastern California, a site that takes eight hours on horseback to reach, newspaper reporter Alan Berry had succeeded in making high-quality cassette tape recordings of bizarre vocalizations coming at night from nearby in the woods. Other than in the form of fleeing shadows through the trees, he and the others at this camp, cowering inside a primitive lean-to, never caught sight of the authors of these sounds, but during the day they did find massive five-toed footprints in the mud, up to eighteen inches long.

Businessman and hunter Ron Morehead joined the project, and was able to collect further clear audio, upping the total take to more than ninety minutes. The sounds include not only the typical wood knocks, howls, and whoop-calls, but also a rich array of other forceful vocalizations—some snarling, bestial, threatening, but many also uncannily speech-like, highly articulated, and all of it strikes the listener as issuing from throats and lungs much more prodigious than their human counterparts. Indeed, in 1978, a year-long study, based at the University of Wyoming, was not only unable to detect any evidence of technical manipulation, but further, Professor R. Lynn Kirlin and Lasse Hertel wrote, "Having analyzed the Berry-Morehead tape recording of purported Bigfoot speech using accepted techniques of signal processing [taking into account pitch, amplitude, etc.], the authors find an average vocal tract length of 20.2 cm. This is significantly longer than for a normal human male. Extrapolation of average estimators, using human proportions, gives height estimates of between 6' 4" and 8' 2"."

"There are some vocalizations on these tapes that sound like juveniles," observes Nelson, "and one that we call 'the big male.' I can say that on Ron's tapes there are at least three distinct individuals. On Al's tape, there are at least two."

Berry and Morehead can be heard, at times, actually calling out to, and receiving responses from, their unseen neighbors across a distance of several hundred feet, the exchange occasionally seeming quite playful and impassioned. The Sasquatch evince a fascinating degree of interest in this tight band of humans, in forging and sustaining contact, a willingness to make their presence plainly known that is extremely rare, but not unheard of, in the history of our two species on the continent.

Not surprisingly, though, the dramatic relationship at that site never escalated into a visual interface or, of course, any sort of closer-range conversation; and it lasted, on and off, only until the late fall of 1974, when one incident put an abrupt halt to all such visitations--the men shot and killed a large black bear who'd been prowling through camp.

Readers can learn a great deal more of the story surrounding these encounters in Morehead's recent release, *Voices in the Wilderness*, and in the 1976 book *Bigfoot*, by B. Ann Slate and Alan Berry.

"They have a much larger range in their vocal abilities," says Nelson. "The resonance is much greater, not even counting when you throw in all the whoops and howls. Just the tone and the resonance of the voice alone is enough to tell me that they are not like any human I have ever listened to on tape, and I can tell you I don't know anyone who has listened to more human voice on tape than I have.

"Five seconds of vocalization might take three hours to transcribe. Very painstaking. And this speech is much too fast for me to imitate. I can enunciate much faster than most people, and I can only get up to maybe half the speed on the tapes, once I've broken down the elements and know them. You just can't hear these morphemes at real time. When you slow it down and you retrieve the sounds out of it, phoneme by phoneme, there are a lot of things that could sound like English words or phrases. But I always have to qualify that statement by saying it's a natural thing for us to recognize or to pick bits and pieces out of any vocalization that we would recognize from our own language. I have sat native Spanish speakers down and had them listen to the tapes and they've heard a lot of Spanish words and phrases. I have had native Japanese people sit down and listen to it. I've played them for a colleague of mine who is a native Farsi—or Persian—speaker. And virtually anyone who listens to it, and at various speeds, can pick out something that they recognize. When we talk about 'cognatic' expressions or words from other languages, we have to be careful to qualify it. At the same time, we can't ignore that. There's one spot on one of the Berry tapes where one creature seems to be responding to the campers and the big male says, 'Be careful now, Prosgut.' And it's very clear to everyone who listens to it, and we've got several spots in the transcripts where it sounds like they're actually calling each other by name, which is incredible, I know.

"Interestingly, on the two tapes, two years apart, we can make out two different dialects. There were some words that were shared, but not many words. I believe we are essentially listening to two different clans, or tribes, or whatever you want to call them. So in general, are there some of the same words in different places in the tapes? Yes. Some of the same morphemes are repeated both in query inflections and on retort. It's horribly difficult, though, to define 'words.' So what we have to refer to is morphemes, which are units of meaning. And yes, they are repeated. We have a good start on a database of morphemes and phonemes, even potential words, and a very short list of possible names, where one creature is calling to another."

Attempting to make sense of a language so foreign that it comes with no known framework, no Rosetta Stone, is called "radical translation." The first order of business, Nelson explains, is to apply "a principle of charity," which assumes that any speaker is not contradicting himself. Another initial assumption is that the language has a grammar. Next, one looks for negation, which is something no other animal is able to execute, except for humans. "You try to establish the units for 'yes' and 'no.' We've done that. In fact, the word for 'no' that I think I've uncovered here is actually 'no.'

Scott Nelson's contribution has been profound—his cataloguing of morphemes from one dialect in the Sierra Nevada Mountains, uttered in the early 1970s, as well as a handful of further morphemes recorded recently, elsewhere in North America, and his assembly of a preliminary "phonetic alphabet." But this analysis and transcription still leave us light-years away from an actual translation of what these towering talkers have to say. Even if we could comprehend this particular burst of speech, the Berry/Morehead tapes only capture what's shouted in a highly atypical setting, in the presence of encroaching men at a hunting camp, rather than shared through the presumably much subtler, wider-ranging articulations of private communal and family life.

Nelson holds out hope for a major interactive breakthrough. "To truly discover them as a people we need contact, to speak with them. One property of language, for something to qualify as a language, is that it be learnable. I think we will be able to learn how to communicate with them someday. I don't think we will ever learn their language fully, because I think secrecy and self-preservation will always be important to them. Again, I can use the example of the Romano Gypsies: I think they will always keep part of their language to themselves. But if nothing else I think Sasquatch will be able to communicate with us through our own language. So it will be an effort on both our parts. We may end up communicating in what we would call a pidgin—half human and half Sasquatch."

"There's one spot on Ron's tape where the female comes out with what very much sounds like English, where she says, 'Are you talking with theem?' And the male very clearly comes out and says, 'No...I...won't.' And very slow; that one you can almost hear in real time.

"There's another one where one creature seems to be talking about the food—on the Berry tape they're offering food essentially throughout the whole tape—and one of the creatures sounds like it's repeating our name for food several times. There's one spot where it says, 'Me wat food plen food,' which is a very close pigeon—just what these creatures *would* speak if they'd assimilated some English from us—for 'I'm watching the food.' And right after that is when another one says, 'Be careful now, Prosgut.'"

"I've come to the conviction," says Nelson, "that, short of a corpse, what greater evidence can you have for the existence of any creature than to have discovered his language, and to have taped it, and transcribed it, analyzed it, and proven that it is indeed a language?"

Back in June of 2010, he sent an open letter to the research community:

> Since our ultimate goal is the recovery of Sasquatch
> Language, I have found it necessary to establish a
> phonetic alphabet and transcription standard (based on
> the transcription of the Berry/Morehead tapes), by
> which the contrast and comparison of all future
> suspected language can be facilitated. To this end, as
> an invaluable tool in the future of Sasquatch Language

research, I am requesting that the attached standard be published on research websites and that it be copied and distributed freely. With this, I am also requesting that local investigators begin using this alphabet as soon as possible to accurately document any perceived Sasquatch Language.

It is my belief that there is nothing more important, at this early stage of Sasquatch Language study, than to standardize the documentation of evidence.

A variation of the English Reformed Phonetic Alphabet is used, as transcribed from the Berry/Morehead Tapes (BMT). The existence of the Sasquatch Being is hereby assumed, since any creature must exist before his language.

The purpose of this is to standardize all future transcription of suspected Sasquatch Language and to facilitate comparison of language articulations by future researchers, the ultimate goal being the recovery of Sasquatch Language.

Sasquatch Language is spoken approximately twice as fast as any known language in most analyzed recordings; therefore, it must be slowed down to be transcribed accurately. 50% of real-time will be the standard. Since this is an unknown language, transcribed for the first time, the grammar and syntax of it, likewise, cannot be known. Since words cannot be known, and only suspected in cognates, Sasquatch utterances will be given as individual morphemes (or syllables). Untranscribable vocalizations such as grunts or screams will be noted with capital letters within parentheses, e.g. (G) or (SC). An abbreviation key follows the phonetics key.

This alphabet is expected to grow as additional verified recordings of Sasquatch Language are collected and analyzed, and new extra-human articulations are documented. For example: The well-documented howls, whoops, growls, screams and whistles of

Sasquatch may someday be found to have linguistic meaning; wood- and rock-knocking or tooth-popping may be found to be encoded. It should not be discounted that manipulated tree, limb and stick formations could be graphic expressions of Sasquatch Language, much like runic or pictographic human writing systems.

With the recovery of Sasquatch Language being the anticipated outcome, cooperation and consensus among language researchers should be the first rule of this study.

Phoneme Key
Ä = a in father
A = a in can
B = b in bib
D = d in did
Ë = a in make
E = e in set
F = f in fife
G = g in gag
H = h in ham
Ï = i in machine, ee in meet
I = i in sit
J = y in yes, i in union
K = k in kite, c in cut
L = l in lull
M = m in mom
N = n in nine
Ö = o in lone
O = o in log
P = p in pipe
R = r in roar
Rr = rolled r, as in Spanish or in Scottish Brogue
S = s in sister
T = t in tight
Ü = u in plume, oo in boot
U = u in run, o in union
V = v in verve

W = w in way
Y = oo in book
Z = z in zebra, s in is
' = glottal stop
c = tongue click, not evident in BMT
> = phoneme drawn out Compound Phonemes
ÄÏ = i in like, y in my
JÜ = as in you, u in fume
KH = ch in Scottish loch, x in Spanish Quixote, x in Russian (khah)
SJ = sh in shirt
TSJ = ch in church
ZJ = z in azure, s in treasure
DZJ = j in jail, g in age
NG = ng in sing
Δ (Greek Delta) = th in then
Θ (Greek Theta) = th in thin

Abbreviation Key
(rt) = transcribed at real-time
(75%) = transcribed at a speed other than 50%
(h) = human vocalization
(1-2m) = one or two words or syllables are missing or inaudible here
(int) = interrogative inflection
(dr) = Inflected as a direct response
(imp) = imperative inflection
(w) = whispered
(q) = very low audibility, quiet, almost imperceptible at normal speeds
(im) = human imitating a creature
(ma) = possible male Sasquatch
(fe) = possible female Sasquatch
(ju) = possible juvenile Sasquatch
(G) = grunt, growl or grumble, possible language
(W) = whistle or squeak, possible language
(SN) = snarl, possible language
(SC) = scream, possible language
(TP5) = tooth pop, number in sequence, possible

language, not evident in BMT
(WK3) = wood knock, number in sequence, possible
    language
(RK4) = rock knock, number in sequences, possible
    language

BERRY TAPE I

Transcribed by R. Scott Nelson
These are the first two pages of this transcription as an
example of the prescribed usage of the alphabet. All of
this speech occurred over the first one minute and
eighteen seconds out of a total of ninety minutes
transcribed for all tapes.

Time	Utterance
0:4.5	(W) (W)
0:8.62	(W) (W) (W)
0:15.11	RAM HO BÄ RÜ KHÄ HÜ
0:16.70	WAM VO HÜ KHÖ KHU'
0:17.52	NÖ U PLÄ MEN TI KHU
0:18.82	NÄR LÄ
0:20.21	NA GÖ KÜ STEP GÄ KÜ BLEM
0:21.25	Ü KÜ DZJÄ
0:21.76	FRrÄP E KHÜK LE
0:22.65	ÜN Ï KÜ O GÜ AKH (int)
0:23.85	DÖ WÄÏ NÖ (dr)
0:24.52	MÜ Ï FWI KÖ PÏ KHU' SJ?
0:31.43	(ma) HU Ö NÖ> KHÄ HÜ
0:32.95	PLEN DÜTSJ TISJ
0:33.61	SÏ DZJAÖ GLÖ PÜ MËKH
0:34.90	PÄ KHÏ KÖ DÜ TÜ SEKSÏ
0:35.88	WA HEP DÜ TSJE DÜ FU HEP
0:36.95	(ma) FI KÜ ÄÏ> KHÜ'
0:44.80	FÄ LIP ÄBÄSJ KHU'
0:45.03	NE VER GÖ ? ÖM KHU'
0:47.03	FÖ WÄ Ï>
0:48.08	WA KHU? KVÄM

0:49.16	ITS KÄÏM VÄR US FO RI ZIS TENS
0:51.27	MÖ> FER BÏ KEN JÄ Ä VÄÖN SÏ
	RYK MI RO GHAP – GÏ GO WYP
0:53.66	MÏ WÄTSJ FYD PLËN FYD NÜ
	AÖ> KHE KHU′
0:55.34	NÖ ÄÏ ÄKHSJ HÜ
0:57.13	(h) Come on, boy.
0:58.04	(h) Come on, let's eat.
1:00.93	BÏ KAER FYL NAÖ PRÖS GYD
01.87	NÖÄ Ö JA LET KHE
02.99	MÖÏ PISJ FE KHE KHU′
(h) Come on.	
1:11.58	KHU BEK
1:12.63	KHËÄ KHU′
1:13.77	Ä LÄF
1:14.46	MÖ VE KHÜ
1:14.86	LAF KHU′
1:15.35	NÖ KHÏÄ
1:16.01	KHÖ VË ÄER ZÏ RÄ KIL WÄ KÜ ′ÜSJ
1:17.49	BÜ GÄ TÄÏSJ KHU′

In the six years since he made this pioneering contribution, Scott Nelson's proposed book on this subject has not appeared. His hope was to be able to include many further, corroborating examples of Sasquatch articulations from a wide range of locations. He has received numerous audio clips—from sites in Alabama, Georgia, Minnesota, Wisconsin, California, The Great Smoky Mountains of Tennessee—that contain some of the same phonemes transcribed from the early 1970s, but none thus far remotely approaches the length and texture of the gold standard, the Berry/Morehead tapes.

We can hope that Nelson will carry his work forward, but in any case, others are fully capable of hunting and gathering in this environment; recall, for instance, M.K. Davis's work on Sasquatch speech on page 22 above, recommended videos 12-19.

"Knowing the nature of language," he has said, "and knowing that one of the biggest concerns for Sasquatch, we assume, is the avoidance of people, what I would have to assume is that Sasquatch speaks an assimilated language that includes Spanish, English and Native American, depending on where they are, but that they also have their own basic language, and that they can speak in more than one language.

"Have I heard Spanish words in Sasquatch language? Yes. Have I heard English words? Yes. Language is a living entity that evolves and changes. In Spain, Spanish is not quite the same in different valleys. So, would Sasquatch in Georgia speak a different dialect from Sasquatch in Washington State? Yeah, we'd have to assume that. But I would say that they also have a common language that they could both understand at the same time. And the only thing that would preclude that from happening is extreme isolation. And we know that Sasquatch is so migratory, so fast, can travel such great distances, that I don't believe that that type of isolation exists for them.

"One property of language, for something to qualify as a language, is that it be learnable. I think we will be able to learn how to communicate with them someday. I don't think we will ever learn their language fully, because I think secrecy and self-preservation will always be important to them. Again, I can use the example of the Romano Gypsies: I think they will always keep part of their language to themselves. But if nothing else I think Sasquatch will be able to communicate with us through our own language. So it will be an effort on both our parts. We may end up communicating in what we would call a pidgin—half human and half Sasquatch."

Whether such utopian communion will ever occur face to face, however, I strongly doubt.

39. The Sasquatch Listening Project

Structure skeptics like to ask, "How can we claim to know that Sasquatch build stick and tree structures until we catch them in the act?" It all comes down to what standards one applies to potential evidence, but it's possible to have standards that are too high, impractically high. I'll explain.

For me, finding *potential* Sasquatch structures is never reason enough to conclude that Sasquatch made them. Finding structures is just Step 1. Step 2 is indispensable: to record and listen to audio in the same forest for many nights (100s of hours), and if wood knocks or obvious vocalizations are captured here at, say, 2:45 AM, then I'm comfortable connecting the two phenomena.

It's not 100% proof, I agree, but it is a "preponderance of evidence." That is, I accept that it's much more likely that the structures in this particular forest were made by Sasquatch than that they were made by people, given a) the audio evidence, b) the fact that most of these structures are not the sort that people tend to make, and c) the fact that they *are* the sort of thing people see throughout North America in the exact areas where Sasquatch are also seen by eyewitnesses. In other words, my process is not $1 + 1 = 2$; it's more like $.95 + .95 = 1.9$, and I'm bullish on rounding up to 2.

Why? Because no other explanation even comes close (are neighborhood children filling the woods with structures *and* knocking and screaming in the middle of the night...or is it that two *separate* groups of our kind are responsible?) and because a conservative refusal to round up to 2 means certain stagnation. To raise one's skepticism to an unrealistically high level halts research progress in its tracks because the odds of achieving, in any given situation, an exhaustive array of incontrovertible proof are vanishingly small if we hold out for such an evidentiary slam dunk. Some think that if, say, wood knocks are heard, they cannot be attributed to Sasquatch unless we see or film the subject producing the sound; if structures are found, we have to catch the subject building them in order to connect the dots; and some even go so far as to say that even enormous, human-shaped, five-toed footprints cannot be linked to Sasquatch unless we observe the prints actually being set down by the very feet in question.

I embrace a healthy skepticism (which is why I always take Step 2: audio), but to insist on an idealistic, purist stance is to "let the perfect be the enemy of the good." Sasquatch research is not, and will never be, a hard science or even a Goodall-style branch of primatology. Why? Because that's just not the nature of the beast. They do not allow us to observe them directly, much less to embed within their societies and interview them in the manner of traditional anthropology. They allow us to study them only indirectly (through signals and clues), and so our new anthropology will have to accommodate itself to this reality. See my video "The New Anthropology: A Practical 2-Step Process for Monitoring your Local Sasquatch Group."

For several years, I have curated a Facebook group called The Sasquatch Listening Project. Because reviewing the files in real time is very labor-intensive, long-term recording in Sasquatch territory has not yet become commonplace; even our leading field researchers don't make it a routine practice. Going forward, I hope, this group will be a hub for our new branch of social science. Professional anthropologists will shun such research like the plague until it no longer spells career suicide.

Therefore, it is up to us—citizen scientists.

"But how do I start?" you may ask. First, find structures. If possible, check out woods beside human sources of electric power, high-tension lines or substations. Alternatively, explore any micro forests, ravines, or greenbelts. Take the Random

Forest Challenge; use Google Earth and point to a spot with your eyes closed; you'll be surprised and delighted by what you find, maybe not the first time, but soon. See "Taking the Random Forest Challenge," "Sasquatch & Serendipity," and for a spectacular instance of what can happen if you begin by noticing subtle signs, *even from your car*, and then follow where they lead, enjoy Colorado Bigfoot's "Giant Bigfoot TeePee Structure, p 1."

As discussed above (p. 191), be alert for "side hustles" (or lateral corroboration): small, simple versions of large, more elaborate structures right beside these structures. Another tip to help you rule out *Homo sapiens'* construction: Except in the case of birches and pines, many branches, limbs, and tree trunks used in structures will have been stripped of their bark. Campers are not likely to spend hours on such a painstaking task. It seems likely that the purpose here is to retard the rotting process, to make the elements of the structures, and thus the whole structures themselves, dry out more quickly and last much longer. (Very commonly, too, you will find that the twigs and branches have all been snapped off of trunks and large limbs— a deliberate act, not the result of any natural process of decay.) A second reason may be that bare wood tends to show up better in the forest when seen against a backdrop of ordinary trees. Finally, Sasquatch probably eat wood (as do gorillas and chimpanzees), and the bark in particular is rich in vitamins, minerals, and medicinal qualities; aspirin, for instance, is derived from willow bark.

Most of the bark removed (photo: LeeAnn Carnegie)

Where signs of Sasquatch appear, capture tons of audio. As I say, among all of the hundreds of researchers currently documenting structures, almost none take the vital extra step of simply leaving a digital recorder overnight. Here's the model I use, excellent at $129; it can be programmed to run for several nights in a row between specified hours.

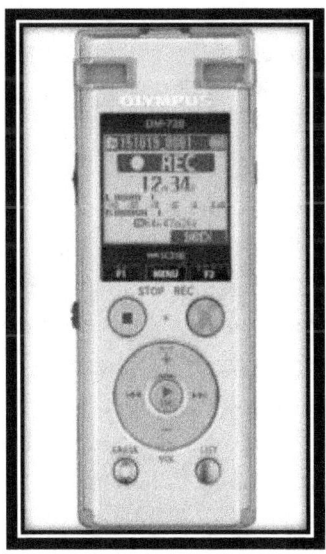

Olympus DM 720

Once your audio recordings and marathon listening sessions begin to repay you with sufficient confidence that the structures were made by Sasquatch, try following in the footsteps of SnowWhiteBigfoot, leaving interesting objects in interesting arrangements at the same spot near the forest day after day, month after month. Your clandestine neighbors will probably notice and return the favor.

On line, stay in touch with our Facebook group discussions, where we will be regularly posting audio clips, techniques, and analytic advances. I hope we can eventually recruit thousands, each of whom will deploy and monitor multiple recorders simultaneously.

I must share with you just what a unique thrill it is to gather audio. You choose a little forest with structures, but it's so dead quiet in here and so close to roads, homes, parks, etc., that you find it literally inconceivable that none other than Sasquatch—*what?!*—will be coming along shortly. When you return to retrieve your recorder, you look around and listen, and it is the exact same silent story among these trees; certainly nothing important can have happened between times. But you hold in your hand proof that, somehow, *much* has happened in between and that in fact you are standing in an empty theater after hours, one that has just played host to startling drama.

See my two videos that chronicle this drama: "At the Sasquatch Keyhole: Six Months, A Micro Forest, and a Good Pair of Headphones" and "Next of Kin Next Door: A Documentary on the New Wave of Sasquatch Research."

In light of Part 4, we will also want to begin keeping track of electromagnetic readings in the most promising locations; here is another type of eavesdropping that will likely teach us indispensable lessons. I have another public Facebook group called Electric Sasquatch, if you are interested in pursuing this angle of inquiry.

After years of searching for an EMF meter that could log data for later review, this one came on the market: the Tenmars TM-192D 3-axis EMF Meter Magnetic Field Meter with Data Logger 30Hz to 2000Hz. It's available on Amazon for less than $200. After downloading a night's readings, you can, with one click, see them in the form of a graph showing flatlines and spikes.

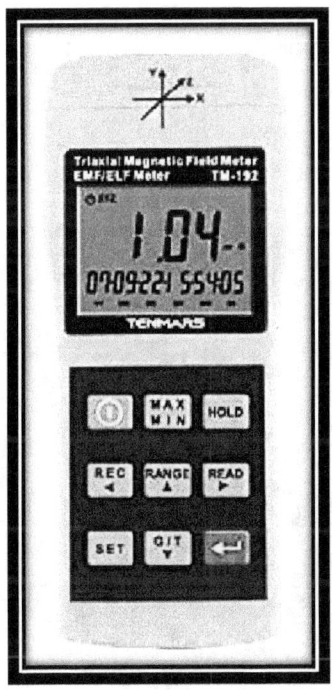

Let's ignite an international movement through the US and Canada.

Once we're up and running with this ambitious venture, the methodological trick will become how best to manage the incoming information flow, to synthesize the disparate sources of archived data, channel new data steadily accumulating, and to analyze all of it such that salient patterns emerge and our knowledge base expands.

I know that many will object vehemently to the very notion of pinpointing Sasquatch, of "filling in the map" of their whereabouts. I share my thoughts in the video "Why Not Just Leave Them Alone? Sasquatch and Civic Duty #3," and Nathan Reo also weighs in on this touchy subject, making the case for why even avid researchers pose no threat to the species. In a mountainous area, he has found numerous scattered hubs or "wallows," his word for spots where—judging from a concentration of stick and tree structures—the local group seems to spend a lot of time. He has drawn a helpful schematic of this system of locations, all of which likely serve as fallback positions when any one position is compromised.

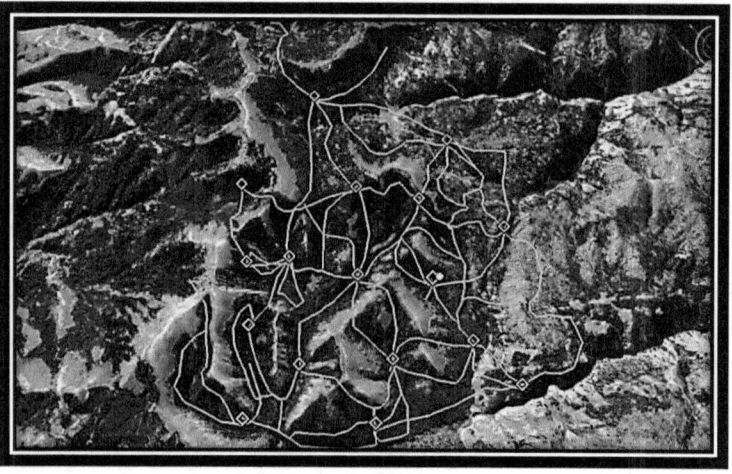

You can listen to him from the 103:40 mark of my video "Next of Kin Next Door." "In between these wallows," Reo explains,

> they'll have tree structures marking their corridors, and if you follow one for long enough, it leads to another wallow. They have a web of corridors throughout the forest. If somebody is approaching this wallow, there's a fight or flight response. They

can choose to be aggressive, or they can choose flight. 99% of the time, they just choose to leave. They'll back right out. A lot of the time, they'll observe you from afar, a couple hundred feet away. They're not these extremely aggressive, territorial animals that everybody teaches that they are. In my experience, they're going to let you walk straight in and look around. They have ample fallback positions. If you invaded a [*Homo sapiens*] camp or hide-out, we would be really territorial. But Sasquatch have so many different places where they can sleep and eat and move throughout the forest…they have fallback positions *for* fallback positions, forward observation posts, recon areas. There's a network of travel ways. If we keep pushing forward, they can retreat and retreat and then loop back around. 100% of the time, this is what I observe.

In other words, our learning curve, our growing awareness of them in any given locale, will not result in the discovery and ruination of their *home*; successful co-evolution alongside us has mandated a decentralized, fluid circulation of *homes*, and this has kept Sasquatch safe across the eons. Our steadily improving knowledge of their proximity and culture won't alter the essential dynamics on the ground; the tactical power imbalance will prevail just because they are incomparably faster and better at eluding us than we are at closing the gap. And if anything, as we gain intimacy via audio recording and general consciousness raising, mainstream society will inevitably come to embrace our next-door neighbors as fellow humans. Though, of course, a small percentage of us will seek to do them harm, the momentum will be, increasingly, toward protective legislation that treats Sasquatch as the indigenous people that they are. In other words, while the first man to kill a "specimen" may become rich and famous, he will also be broadly reviled and will cause lawmaking to accelerate such that the second murderer will spend his life in jail...or worse.

At the macro level, an analogy to our listening project already exists in the realm of astronomy. Volunteers are helping to scan the heavens.

> The International Centre for Radio Astronomy Research (ICRAR) is set to launch the Square Kilometer Array, a "citizen science" application based on computing technology developed at Oxford University. The application, dubbed "theSkyNet" by Australian researchers, would grant anyone not affiliated with the global telescope project access to the datasets formed out of the Array's work. (Computerworld Australia)

> The SKA will consist of 3000 radio dishes, spread as far as 2000 miles in every direction from a central core. (PopSci.com)

Let's compare these 3000 dishes, cast skyward, to countless digital ears placed respectfully in the forests across the land. Let us reclaim our childlike wonder.

Here we go.

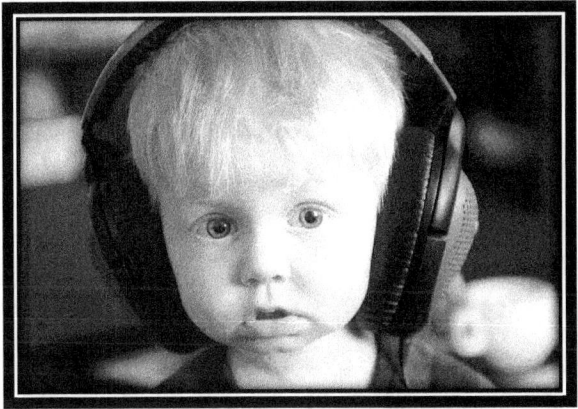

Cover illustration by Warren Port. Port is a self-taught Artist and Illustrator residing in Dorset, England, with a life-long interest in Sasquatch.

Cover design by Dale Boswell.

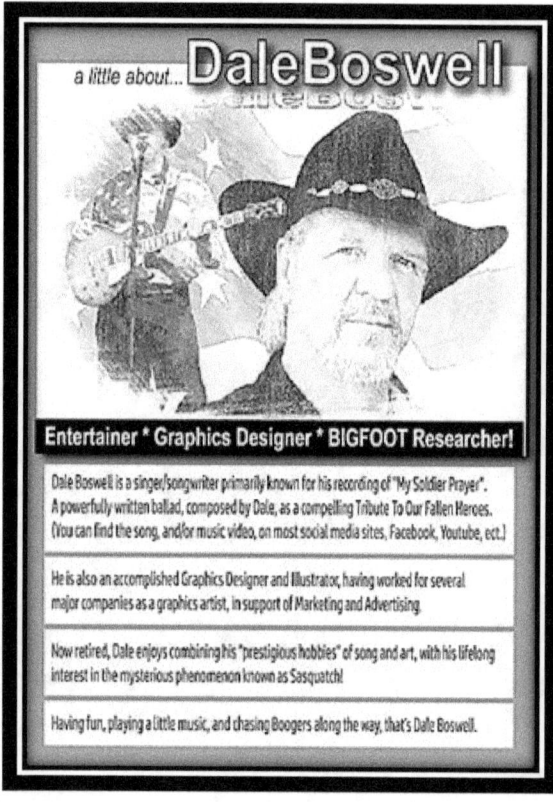

www.ingramcontent.com/pod-product-compliance
Lightning Source LLC
Chambersburg PA
CBHW071331280526
45787CB00001B/60